Riding the Tiger

A Mediator's Tale and Guide

Will Mooser

Lulu Publishing Services rev. date: 10/30/2019

This book is dedicated to
Dr. Ronald Spinka.

Mentor, Friend & Confidant

CONTENTS

PREFACE

We humans generally want predictability: a safe, secure job, a stable marriage and a car that consistently starts.

Throughout our lives we develop methods or roles, e.g., victim, aggressor, passive aggressor, defensive anger, denial and many others to achieve control and thus predictability. Some turn to drugs or alcohol to achieve a predictable state of consciousness.

Conflict, by its very nature, is profoundly destabilizing and unpredictable. Mediators refer to their work of seeking harmony out of this quagmire of emotional instability as "riding the tiger."

I ride that Tiger.

ACKNOWLEDGEMENTS

First, to my wife and partner, Susan. What would I do without you? It goes beyond thanks … must be love. Thank you.

Second, to my mentors, Mr. Ron Kelly, Mr. John Ford, Ms. Chris Knowlton and Ms. Harriet Whitman-Lee. Thank you most of all for your help on this path that makes such a difference in my life and in our world.

Third, to all the people who have helped me in this endeavor: Ms. Stacy Waters for all the editorial help she has given; my family and friends, who put up me; and for all of those that follow the peacemakers' path.

A LETTER FROM THE BENCH

April 3, 2009
RE: Mr. Will Mooser

TO WHOM IT MAY CONCERN:

I am the Commissioner who regularly hears two small claims calendars each week in the Hayward Hall of Justice. I have had this assignment since 2006. Beginning in 2007, I was also assigned to the civil restraining order calendars. Will Mooser has been a volunteer mediator throughout this time, along with numerous other volunteers through SEEDS community mediation program. These volunteers provide mediation services on the day of court for both small claims and civil harassment restraining order calendars, and they have become an integral and essential part of the adjudication process on these calendars.

Mr. Mooser has proven to be not only an extremely reliable and dedicated volunteer, but he is by far the most effective mediator. His rate of success in helping litigants come to agreements is nothing less than astonishing. The courtroom clerk and one of the departments where Mr. Mooser volunteers reports a 98% success rate. I attribute this to his extraordinary skills and to his personality, which seems to draw out the best in people and to enable them to see beyond their immediate situation. I have known him to stick with a set of litigants through several mediation sessions and even through several different sets and types of claims in court until a final resolution is reached.

I recommend Mr. Will Mooser as a mediator whose skills and effectiveness are, in my experience, unsurpassed.

L. Thomas Surh
Superior Court
State of California
County of Alameda

INTRODUCTION

Mediation is magic. I once had a judge ask me, "What in the world are you doing in there, sprinkling them with pixie dust?" I could only answer, "I listen and connect with the parties in conflict and help them define what they need to transition from conflict." In this book I will attempt to explain that magic by addressing the techniques I used in the court to be a successful mediator.

I had taken training in mediation at the University of California, Berkeley, from Ron Kelly. At the end of the training I decided that mediation was what I wanted to spend the rest of my life doing. I was at a transition point in my own life, searching for my next step: What did I want to accomplish in this next stage? What would be my future identity? I had spent years working to put a roof over my family's head and to put food on the table. Now I had the opportunity to figure out my larger purpose. Through mediation training I had found a role that not only intrigued and fascinated me, but also seemed to fit my naturally observant temperament and abilities.

I immersed myself in my mediation work. I mediated in the California Superior Court in the Civil, Small Claims and Civil Harassment divisions. At the community level, working through SEEDS Community Resolution Center, I handled individual cases as well as cases for the cities of Berkeley and Hayward. I developed a private mediation practice and began presenting at conferences and mediation training programs. To carry the message forward, I joined the board of directors of the Association for Dispute Resolution of Northern California, eventually serving as their Treasurer, and, later, Board President. Through that work, I was able to connect with the larger mediation community through our national parent organization, the Association for Conflict Resolution. Through that work, I got involved in the American Bar Association's Psychology of Conflict Resolution committee. My new path was set.

The chapters in this book cover twelve mediation cases that I handled in the California Superior Court, Small Claims Division, where I worked almost every Friday for more than three years. I usually mediated three to five successful cases per day, a success rate that surprised many of my court colleagues. This work was one of the most fulfilling things I have ever done: being a peacemaker. And as my mediation trainer Ron Kelly once told me, "We need all the peacemakers we can get."

I present these stories in a case study format, describing actual events that took place in my mediation work.* My intention is to demystify the mediation process, making it approachable, usable, and successful.

Conflict is, after all, just the need for change.

* All names, dates, specific dollar amounts, places, and specifics that might otherwise reveal a party's identity have been changed or omitted in order to comply with mediation confidentiality laws and to protect the privacy of the people involved.

MESMERIZED

Each of us must admit to a drive for self-preservation, especially when confronted with conflict. Toward that goal we develop coping techniques to optimize our power in interpersonal contacts, enhance our perception of personal control in life's situations, and increase our options for our future. These techniques are often learned when we are very young, solidified as we mature, and utilized throughout our lives. Some people choose to characteristically adopt a meek, accommodating posture, while others may be overtly forceful and domineering. Some use "mesmerizing" (capturing the attention of others by using energized body and voice) as a way of gaining control.

This was my fourth case of the day. I had just returned from my usual lunch of a sandwich in the Safeway parking lot, where I thought about the meaning of my role as mediator. I was happy to be giving my time and my life to make a difference in people's lives.

As I entered the courtroom, Dave, the bailiff, nodded and called me over. "Well, we have an interesting case here, Will. Both these guys said they would like to have a mediation. How about it?"

I smiled. "Sure, I'll go talk to them."

I looked over at the two men that Dave had pointed to in the gallery. The plaintiff, a white man in his mid-thirties, was casually dressed in jeans, t-shirt, sneakers and denim work jacket, looking as if he had come from a job site. The other, an African American man in his sixties, wore a tailored blue denim pants suit with flared legs and gold chains. He was dressed for court, in a flashy, 1970's sort of way. It had been a long time since I'd seen that look.

I smiled. *Yes, Dave, very interesting,* I thought to myself.

I walked over to the African American man and established eye contact. "Hi. My name is Will. I work as a mediator in this court, and I've been told that you would be willing to mediate your case."

"Yeah. I'd like to do that," he said. "I'm sure I'm right about this. This guy has not fulfilled his contract, not completed the job, and so I don't owe him any money for a job that's unfinished."

"I can understand that. Why pay for something that hasn't been finished? Would you be willing to talk with him about it?"

"Yeah. I'll talk with him about it. But I wanna make sure I maintain my rights."

I agreed, "That's right. You gotta to make sure about that. If we don't reach an agreement, then you can come back to see the judge."

I approached the plaintiff and said, "I've just talked to the other side and he's willing to go to mediation … you know, to talk about it. Would you be willing to do that?" The white man was still on the step. He didn't like being in court. It was clear he felt aggrieved and wanted his money. This was easy to read by the anxious vibes that he gave off: uncertain but wanting a resolution. He looked down and sighed. "All right. I want to be the best person I can be, you know. I want to be fair."

I felt optimistic. I knew from my previous mediation experiences that agreeing to mediate is the first positive step in the whole process. Getting the consent of all parties is also critical. No mutual resolution is possible without it.

I gathered the parties together at the back of the courtroom after the roll call and swearing-in and motioned to Jim, the court clerk, that I was taking them to the empty jury gathering room on the third floor, where mediators frequently worked. As we walked to the elevator I walked in front, the unspoken leader. It's important to take the lead right from the start.

When we reached the jury gathering room, I guided them to a well-lit corner, sat down, and began my standard introduction to the mediation process.

I asked whether either of them had been through mediation before. Neither had. Then I explained how the process would work, what we would do, and my ground rules, while establishing eye contact and gaining consent from each. I then ended with the most important rule: *No interrupting.*

"When you interrupt, you are not fully listening to the other party. I, on the other hand, can interrupt with questions like, 'Did I understand you correctly?' or to clarify points for my own understanding. Now ... I always start with how we will address each other. My name is Will."

With a gentle hand movement, I signaled to the younger man, the plaintiff, who replied, "My name is Jeff."

Again, with a gentle hand movement I signaled to the defendant. "My name is T.J., at least that's what everyone calls me."

I began by questioning the plaintiff, asking him why he had brought suit. Starting with this question is important because sometimes defendants don't even know why they are there, and they need an understanding of the complaints against them.

Jeff replied quietly, "I have a small company that puts in liner swimming pools. T.J. contacted me to do a job for him in the Oakland hills. I did the job at a discounted rate because he explained to me that he was retired and on disability and couldn't afford my usual rates. We came to an agreement at a discounted price, and I started working."

"Did he give you a deposit?" I asked.

"Yes, he did."

"How much?"

"About thirty percent."

I took notes on my legal pad. "Please ... continue."

"We had to hand-dig the whole pool." Jeff looked at his hands folded stiffly in his lap. He spoke in a soft voice, as if reciting what he had been thinking about. He shook his head. Almost plaintively, he said, "I can't understand why T.J. didn't pay me. We did the job, and then he wouldn't even answer my phone calls."

I raised my hand and asked, "Did you have a signed contract for the work?"

"Yes," he replied. "Here it is." He handed me a single sheet of paper. I glanced at the contract and asked him to continue.

Jeff described how his workers had dug the hole for a swimming pool, put in the liner, installed the steps, curb, and ladder, filled the pool, then verified that it had no leaks. He had accomplished what he thought was a good job. He had received a third of his payment at the start of this work and couldn't understand why — despite repeated phone calls — he had not received the balance.

As his story continued, I found his perspective extremely naïve. I had worked as a licensed California contractor for decades and knew the standard business practices in this industry. I asked him if he had filed liens against the property. He had not. Had he kept accurate records of the time he had spent on the job? He had not. Had he taken any notes or invoiced for any of the additional work he claimed he had done? He had not. As I looked at the contract, I saw that almost all the standard legal boilerplate of modern construction contracts was entirely absent.

His explanation was short, taking about five minutes.

I turned to the defendant, T.J., and said, "You're up!"

And boy did T.J. launch!

"Man, I can't believe this shit! I've done all I can do! I trusted this guy! I bent over *backwards* to help him do his job! His workers would show up and not even know about the changes that I had talked to Jeff about on the phone just the night before! This is so fucked up!" He threw his hands into the air in a gesture of heated exasperation and sat back in his chair with a loud sigh, then leaned forward again to continue.

I held up my hand quickly. "Let's watch the language." Profanity can often inflame tensions or intimidate the other party, and therefore is generally not helpful to the mediation process.

T.J. still had the floor. I could tell already that he was only at the beginning. He continued his heated story, forcefully waving his arms and speaking in a loud voice as he described the constant delays and shoddy work he had endured. His gestures were excessively animated in his attempts to take the floor, but I could recognize his frustration.

A piece of the puzzle was missing for me though, as I couldn't understand what had happened toward the end of the project. T.J. was vague.

"Well, I wasn't happy about a lot of things! These guys didn't do what they were supposed to do."

"Like what?" I asked.

"They came in and they didn't put in my steps right. They wouldn't even show up until midday. They trampled my plants, and they didn't put all the dirt where I told them to. Man, they just didn't do the job right! *I'm* the victim here!"

I listened intently, taking notes and gradually comprehending his story. Glancing up, I could see that he was not yet finished.

He continued forcefully, "I'm on disability, man, and living on a limited budget. I just can't put up with this shit! I've worked hard *all my life*, supported my wife and kids ... now I gotta deal with this shit! It's not fair. It's just wrong, and I'm not going to put up with it!" He paused. "I finally had to lock the gate on them!"

I was surprised. "You locked them out?" I asked him quizzically.

"Yeah, man, I had no choice!"

I glanced at Jeff. He was completely captivated. Slack-mouthed and spellbound, he was mesmerized by T.J.'s masterful showmanship.

I realized that T.J. was trying, either consciously or unconsciously, to take charge of the mediation. By using exaggerated, highly energized vocal patterns and tempo, giant hand gestures, and varied body postures, he was attempting to establish his power and control in a situation that otherwise felt intimidating to him. He reminded me somewhat of an evangelist preacher in the way he grabbed and held attention. Jeff was clearly overwhelmed and intimidated by T.J.'s domineering stance.

Mediators frequently refer to the use of drama and intimidation like this as "hijacking" the mediation. While such techniques do frequently function in the real world to shift conflict in some way (which is why such behavior is quite common), in a situation where a mutual resolution is sought, the mediator *must* understand such behavior and keep it in reasonable check for the comfort of all parties, as well as for achieving final resolution.

As usual, I had been taking notes, glancing at T.J. from time to time and nodding that I was listening. At the next pause, I broke in to take charge of the spiraling situation.

"Okay, yes, the pool had been put in, only a third paid for and no leaks. So, why haven't you paid the balance?" I asked, getting to the heart of the matter.

T.J. stood up quickly and began to nervously pace back and forth in front of us, claiming that he had been put into a diminished position. Again, using expansive hand and arm gestures and speaking loudly and rapidly, he continued, "Man, I cannot believe this shit! This guy hasn't fulfilled his contract, hasn't completed his work, hasn't put the steps in right, and just hasn't been a good contractor!"

He paused, then continued, "Plus, he has some workers who were looking pretty closely at my pot plants. I don't want them ripping me off! And I wasn't happy with the steps he put in."

This seemed a crucial admission, the transition point at which T.J. was becoming transparent about one of the hinges in this conflict. He had a crop of marijuana plants that he'd probably not want to mention to a judge. (This case took place prior to California's legalization of marijuana.)

I called a caucus, a process whereby the mediator talks with each party separately and in private. During a caucus, if I discuss something with the party that might facilitate an agreement, I always ask for consent by saying, "Can I share this with the other party?"

I chose to talk to Jeff first, since he had spoken for five minutes and T.J., almost fifteen. I also thought that Jeff was the most uncertain about what was happening, and I wanted to give T.J. a break, hoping he would simmer down a bit. I asked T.J. if he would step out into the hall. He agreed, and he left.

"Jeff, thank you for agreeing to do this. I know it's hard when you get to court, and everything seems to be hanging in the balance." I paused. "Please realize that I'm only here to help the parties understand each other. Now please tell me honestly, what is going on with *you*?"

He was at a loss. Staring at the floor, he started into his story. "I just don't understand this guy. We came in and did the job. He would phone me every night and complain about things, and I even did the job at a discounted price. I just don't know what to do. There was no making him happy."

I was quiet for a few minutes. He was unwinding and needed time to relax.

"Jeff," I asked, "where are you from and how did you get started in this business?" I was bringing him back to familiar ground.

Smiling and relaxing a bit, he responded, "Well, I'm from Montana. I married a girl from this area and because there was no work for me in Montana, we came down here. We're living with her family now until we get our feet on the ground."

He paused, then continued, "I just don't understand this guy. It's like he doesn't even hear me. I did all the work, put up with all kinds of shit and now he won't pay me. I've got all my sub-contractors and suppliers on me now, and I've got bills that have to get paid."

"Yeah," I said, "I can understand that. I've been a licensed contractor since 1973. It's a tough business."

I paused, while he realized that I understood him and what he was going through. This was a transformative moment for him.

"Jeff," I began, "As a licensed contractor I noticed that the forms you are using are not the current ones necessary to work in California. I also noticed that your contractor's license number was not listed on the forms and that you received more than the standard ten percent of the contract price to start the job. We are talking privately now, so you need not be afraid that I will disclose this to the other side. Because we are talking in confidence, can you tell me what is going on?"

Jeff was quiet, nodding his head up and down as he gained courage to open up to me.

"Okay, I'm not a licensed contractor. But I did the work as per the codes! I'm an honest man, and I'm just trying to support my family."

Quietly I asked, "How do you think the judge will look at the fact that you are not licensed?"

Hanging his head, he said, "I don't know ... I only want what is fair."

We sat in silence for a few moments, and then I said, "Well, let me go talk to the other side."

I went into the hallway and motioned T.J. to sit down on one of the benches there. "Well, T.J., how are you doing?" "Man, I just can't believe this shit! I'm the one wronged here. He didn't finish the job." He had calmed down somewhat. I sat on the bench, my presence calm, and made eye contact as an equal. He shook his head, then started in again, "Man, how is a black man gonna get a break? This shit is so wrong!"

As I watched, he got up again and started pacing back and forth in front of me, again using expansive hand gestures and exaggerated vocal modulation. As he was doing this, he kept glancing at me to see my reaction.

I just remained seated, radiating calm, and listened. After a few minutes of this, he suddenly stopped mid-sentence and mid-stride. He looked at me questioningly.

I just smiled and said, "Hey man, I was raised in Oaktown ...with the brothers. That shit don't cut no ice with me."

This was a transformative moment for him, when his world met my world. Sighing, smiling, and somewhat deflated, he sat down next to me and said quietly, "Yeah, I could tell you weren't no hater." We sat for a moment in silence, knowing that we were in concert, connected, together in the moment as equals.

I then asked, "Okay, man, we gotta move forward on this. How we gonna do that?"

Because we had established reciprocal communication, T.J. felt that he could be heard. "Okay, I've got my pot plants that are about to be harvested. His workers were looking them over. They were gonna rip me off, like I just knew it! The job took longer than they said it would, and my harvest time is almost here."

"How long before you bring your crop in?" I asked.

"I need another four weeks."

I asked for clarification. "So, anything that happens has to be five weeks from now."

"Yeah. Five'll work."

"Are you willing to pay Jeff what is owed? I mean, what do you think the judge would say about you locking him out and not paying your bill?"

"Yeah, five weeks. I'll have the funds to pay him."

"So, can I go back to him and tell him you are ready to settle and pay your bill if he does the corrections, but you want him to start in five weeks?" We agreed to the date on the calendar. "Will you have a check in the amount owed when he finishes?"

"Yeah. That'll work," T.J. said.

"Okay. I'll go talk to Jeff then."

I returned to Jeff, who was now standing in the jury gathering room staring out the window.

"Okay, Jeff. I think we have a deal."

He looked suddenly relieved, his world shifting from feeling lost to finding a new direction in life. "What can I do? I want out of this so bad!"

"It's okay, man, we got it," I said. Leading him to a quiet seating area nearby, I continued, "Can you be on site five weeks from now to do the work? Can you have it done in three days? If you can, then you will get your check for the full amount" — then I struck a serious tone with firm eye contact — "but you have to agree in a legal document to do this. As will he. I don't want to create a document that you can't fulfill." In the court mediation process the document of agreement is legally binding.

Jeff, now happy and relieved, said, "Of course I can do that. I just want to finish this job and get paid!"

"Okay, so I'm going to write up this mediated agreement." I pointed to my notes. "Do you understand that you will be legally bound to complete this agreement?" It's always a good idea to reconfirm any legally binding details.

"Oh, yes! Just get me out of this."

I went back and forth between them — they were still separated — and established the work yet to be done, the start date, the completion date, the money owed, and the receipts to be provided, while continuing to ensure that each of the men felt recognized and heard. At the end of this process I brought them together to sign the agreement. Both had accepted that it was over, yet T.J. launched again into his hypnotic, mesmerizing patter.

I held my hand up, looked him straight in the eye and said, "Hey, man, I thought we weren't gonna do that anymore."

He stopped, smiled, chuckled and nodded his head in assent, and we quietly returned to the courtroom to officially submit the agreement.

The full story of this case started with Jeff being late to start the job. Jeff was a novice and was in over his head in an industry in which he wasn't fully competent, and he wasn't even sure how to be. Unlicensed as a contractor, he was also using unknown workers from the nearby labor *pickup spots, paying them $10 per hour and charging the customer $25 an hour per laborer. The workers had indeed spotted T.J.'s pot plants. T.J., meanwhile, had been counting on the money from the proceeds of these plants to fund the pool work, and had been scared by the workers stealthily eyeing the plants as if they were planning to steal them. Both Jeff and T.J. had something to lose by a potential full disclosure in a litigious courtroom setting. Mediation, on the other hand, proved to be the best option for both parties to move forward in a win-win capacity. Everyone felt the terms were fair, and both were pleased with the agreement.*

FROM THE TOOL BOX

1. One of the most successful techniques I used in this case was the use of the caucus, a private meeting with each party. When we are at the mediation table, I demand the strict rules of court. This creates a formal setting. In caucus it becomes informal, allowing parties to disclose their information without fear of the other party.

2. With each of the parties I established a "cultural" connection. In one it was as a professional contractor. In the other it was my own cultural ethnicity that allowed bonds of understanding, trust and unity.

3. A third technique I used was to periodically reaffirm that we had a deal in process. This is a common technique in mediation, serving to reinforce each party's faith in the mediation process, to validate his or her efforts, and to encourage each party to continue working toward an agreement.

4. Lastly, I made use of silence and pauses. This technique allows time for the party to think about what has been said and to formulate answers at his or her own pace. It also places the responsibility on the party for continuing the conversation.

──── DOING A ONE-EIGHTY ────

People don't always tell the whole truth in mediation. Perhaps a party feels that he or she can get away with something, that by not bringing the complete truth forward it will remain hidden in the shadows.

People might also bend the truth to suit their own needs, using offense as a defense. Denial is a human trait, one that we all are guilty of at one time or another. This case touches on all these nuances of evasion.

It was a busy Friday morning with 28 cases on the courtroom calendar. The afternoon was even busier, with more than 60 cases spread out through two different courts. We had three mediators working that morning, and I was the last one to get a case. My case involved two young men who had a disagreement regarding an apartment rental in a local housing complex.

The plaintiff was a white guy in his late twenties. His flashy-yet-smart jacket and tie gave him a cocksure appearance that was hard to miss yet still within the bounds of suitable courtroom attire.

He sure looks confident in his case, I thought.

The defendant, the property manager of the complex, was about the same age, also white, and he was dressed more casually in a light jacket and jeans. He was quiet in his approach and attitude, but he also exuded a calm sense of confidence. He looked prepared, carrying a large file in his hands.

To begin our mediation, we headed to the witness room, a

cramped, sparsely furnished space with no windows situated near the entrance doors to the courtroom. Entering the lock code with a series of rapid clicks, I opened the door, gestured both parties in, and took a seat in the chair between them.

After my standard introduction about the mediation process, I asked them to exchange documentation with each other to understand the other's evidence for their case. In a small claims court, each party has the right to review the other side's evidence before going to trial.

They obligingly exchanged paperwork. The plaintiff glanced dismissively through the large, manila file he was given, while the defendant carefully flipped through the few loose papers handed to him.

"My name is Will. How would you like to be addressed?" I asked the parties.

I motioned to the plaintiff with an upturned palm. "I'm Anthony," he replied, "but you can call me Tony. I rented the apartment."

"I'm Bill, and I represent the rental company that rented the apartment," the defendant responded.

Good! We're on a first-name basis, I thought, smiling at the two men.

Getting down to business, I asked the property manager, "Bill, do you have the full authorization from the rental company to enter into a settlement of this claim?" In cases like this one involving company representation, it is important to establish that a party has such authorization before moving forward with the case.

"Yes," he answered quickly and directly, "I have full authorization."

Having ensured eligibility for the mediation process, I started with the plaintiff as I always do, saying, "I really don't know anything about your case. Would you please tell me what brought you to court today?"

Tony smiled and began, "I rented an apartment from these people, and they have not returned my security deposit. I have done everything I need to do to prove my claim." Placing his hand firmly on his stack of papers, he continued sternly, "They have lied to me."

I held up my hand and said, "Let's be respectful." Accusations are never a positive starting point.

Still smiling, Tony continued, "They have not followed the law by returning my deposit on time. The apartment was left in good condition, and I have photos to prove it. I've gone online and gotten all the information I need to prove my claim."

He then went into detail about how the management company had failed to give him an initial walkthrough after renting the apartment. There had also been no final inspection when he left. He had given his 30 days' notice, had moved out and had returned his keys to the manager's office. Digressing from the main details, he recounted how the laundry machines never worked and how other tenants had sometimes taken his parking place. He also complained about how the grounds were unkempt and how other tenants were unhappy with the complex.

I had been taking notes and glancing at Bill, the apartment manager, from time to time. Though he had begun the proceedings with a demeanor of nonchalance, Bill had become increasingly tense and quiet. As Tony went down his long list of complaints, Bill shook his head in disgust as he stared angrily at the floor.

I said to Tony, "Well, I can see you've really done your homework."

"Oh yes, and I've written everything up for the judge to see just how these people have tried to take advantage of me."

Bill looked as if he were about ready to come unglued. He had been following the rules of the mediation: no interrupting, no "shaking of fists or rolling of eyes," and silently waiting for his turn to speak, but I could tell it was taking a toll. I glanced at him reassuringly several times to try to calm him.

I asked Tony, "Did you show Bill this paper when you exchanged your paperwork?"

"No, I must have forgotten it," Tony responded.

"Well, as I said earlier, each side has the right to see what the other side is going to show the judge. If you are going to use that to establish your case, Bill has to see it first."

Taking it from him, I slid the paper across the table, and Bill picked it up to read. "This is a lie." He shook his head in disbelief.

I held up my hand and said, "As we have agreed, there will be no disrespect allowed at this table. I can understand, Bill, that you might not agree with what is being said, and to be honest, this setting is the perfect place to discuss the issues." It was important to re-establish these respectful parameters. Stopping insults before they get rolling keeps a mediation running smoothly. I then proceeded. "I'm really curious to hear your side of this. You have been waiting to speak. Please do so now."

Bill sighed and began, "Tony rented this apartment last year and signed a one-year lease." He opened his file and leafed through the papers, one at a time, pointing at each document and explaining how it proved his case. "Here is the rental agreement and attached is the apartment inspection record at the time of rental. You can see here at the bottom where Tony signed it. Please also see that there was no parking space rented by him."

I glanced over at Tony, but he was looking away sheepishly.

Bill continued. "The apartment was in very good condition, freshly painted, and the carpets were new. Here are the receipts for those carpets. The complex has a no-pet rule, but Tony had a girlfriend with a pit bull that she would bring over on the weekends. I have received numerous complaints from the neighbors about this." He produced a stack of papers, the completed complaint forms that tenants had given to management. "I had to talk to Tony a number of times about this, and he would say he'd do something about it, but he never did."

Bill appeared to have all his ducks in a row, and he appeared to be gaining confidence in the process.

"As far as a thirty-days' notice, we never got anything from Tony."

Tony interrupted, "I told the secretary!"

I held up my hand. "Tony, we agreed at the beginning that there would be no interrupting. Bill let you have your time. Now it's his turn."

Bill resumed. "We never got anything in writing. The keys were never returned, and so we had to change the locks. Also, when we entered the apartment, we found that the dog had crapped on the carpets, and they had to be replaced. Here is the bill for that."

I looked over at Tony, but he would not meet my questioning look.

"Here is the statement from us as to the security deposit and how it was used up in the repairs necessary to return the apartment to a rentable condition. As you can see, it is unopened, the date mailed is within the twenty-one-day period necessary by law, and it is marked 'return to sender.' The forwarding address that Tony had left with the post office was invalid."

At this point Tony was fidgeting in his seat and avoiding all eye contact.

Bill seemed to be finished, so I spoke up.

"Gentlemen, I'd like to remind you both that when you were sworn in, you swore to tell the truth in these proceedings. I'm sure that both of you would want to be careful not to perjure yourself since the penalties for doing so would far exceed the couple of thousand dollars that are on the table."

Tony was staring at the table, looking dead serious. *Yes, a court of law is some serious stuff indeed,* I mused as I looked at him earnestly.

"I'm also sure that the judge will review all your paperwork and will make his ruling based on the evidence presented. This is, after all, an evidence-based system. I would suggest that both of you" — I looked solemnly at Tony — "review the paperwork, think about your side of this case, and make your decision *very carefully* about what would be best for you."

I paused for a few moments, then asked, "Will either of you reconsider your position in this lawsuit?"

"No," was the decided response from both parties.

I sighed. "In that case we'll have to return to court."

This case did not settle in mediation. It was returned to the courtroom to be heard before the judge. The tale that unfolded in court was very different than the one I had heard. Tony had changed his story by 180 degrees. He realized that Bill's meticulous evidence meant his case was far from airtight.

The judge ruled for the defendant, meaning that it was the judgment of the court that the plaintiff had failed to prove his case. This provided the document of resolution that Bill needed to give to his bosses, the property owners. It also established that Tony could not reopen the case for further lawsuits in this matter.

Perhaps Tony felt that he had paid the court fees, shown up at court and would roll the dice and see what would happen. It was difficult to understand how he could have thought he would win. He lost.

FROM THE TOOL BOX

1. I believe that the mediator is, in fact, working for both parties to help them better understand each other's side of their conflict. Usually when parties become aware of evidence held by the other side, they are more willing to come to a compromised agreement. In fact, hundreds of cases I have mediated were settled in this way.

2. When such resolutions happen, both parties request a dismissal of the case and agree that they will bring no further legal action before the court regarding the matter at hand.

— GUNSHOTS AND GARDENING —

This difficult case came to me through another court mediator. Weeks before, the court had granted the parties' earlier request for a continuance to gather more facts. The original mediator was due to be overseas at the time of the new court date, so he filled me in on the case details and I took the reins.

This case demonstrates the profound shift of personal outlook — what I also refer to as the "transitional moment" — that can occur when the mediator provides the disputants with sharper insights or a better solution than they had previously thought possible. The promise of disputants having both financial and psychological needs met is precisely why mediation is so much more appealing than courtroom litigation.

When I arrived at court that morning, Jim, the court clerk, told me the case that had been passed to me was on the current day's calendar and that both parties were present. I learned that we would be going to the jury room after the parties were sworn in. Jim, as competent as ever, had husbanded the process through by swearing the parties in, letting the judge in his chambers know that we were going into mediation and then waving us forward. Without competent people like Jim, the court system would be lost.

I gathered the parties — who appeared to be starkly different kinds of people from one another — into the jury room. The plaintiff, looking like a well kempt academic, wore a jacket and tie, a sweater vest, comfortable shoes and neatly-pressed slacks. The defendants were a couple, a husband and wife team. The man was dressed casually in jeans, work boots, flannel shirt and denim jacket. He was bearded and had the blackened, grease-stained hands of a mechanic. The woman meant business, but not in a corporate kind of way. She wore tight-fitting black pants, black high-heeled boots, white blouse, black tux jacket and heavy makeup.

Wow, no wonder there's a fight going on here! I thought. I couldn't help but notice the many differences in class and personal background that their self-presentations suggested, and I wondered how these folks would ever manage to find common ground.

I surmised that the academic intellectual was accustomed to having a standard of predictable control of his world. His demeanor told me that he was not only uncomfortable being in conflict, but very angry with what had happened.

The husband and wife were blue-collar, salt-of-the-earth folks. He was used to controlling his world through working with his hands and was more comfortable with direct dialogue. He also seemed a little resentful at being called into court, a world that was both unfamiliar and threatening. She was the calmest member of the group, though her fear of the underlying menace of a court judgment against her and her husband was plain to see. Her eyes darted quickly around the table, only to return to quietly staring down.

I asked the parties to sit across from each other while I sat at the head of the table and began the process.

"I understand there was a continuance granted in this case. Unfortunately, the original mediator is not able to attend this meeting since he had to travel overseas. Therefore, he requested that I take over this case. Is this change agreeable to you both?"

Both parties agreed. I took the court forms out, added my name and the current trial date and had each person initial it. I then explained how the mediation process works and that they would hopefully work out an agreement that would benefit them all.

I was establishing myself as the leader in the process to lead them out of conflict.

"Although you have already signed an Agreement to Mediate and the process of mediation has been explained to you, I would like to go through just a few of my ground rules."

They all nodded in acceptance. I then explained my ground rules: no disrespect, no eye rolling, no fist shaking and no interrupting.

I explained how the mediation process works and that we would hopefully work out an agreement that would benefit them all. They all agreed.

"I don't really know much about your case. I know it might be an inconvenience for you to repeat the details, but could you please tell me about it? It would help me to hear the case in your own words. After all, I'm here to try to help you solve this problem, and the better I can understand it, the more I can help you."

I signaled with an outstretched palm to the plaintiff — the subdued academic — to begin.

"Well, this is about a property rental. It was my parents' home, and I rented it to these people."

The plaintiff looked at the other party who then nodded in agreement and continued. "I rented it to them almost seven years ago, and when they left, the property was trashed. Look at these pictures!"

He had a stack of about 30 eight-by-ten-inch photos that he pushed forward on the table. I didn't look at them but motioned him to continue.

"They totally destroyed the place, and now I've got to get all of these things fixed!"

He was noticeably upset — probably an unfamiliar state for him. I was using my best calming manner, meeting him eye-to-eye and nodding for him to continue.

After allowing several moments of silence while he composed himself, I said, "I'm really sorry that this is happening and that you find yourselves here. I'm sure we can find a way out of this."

Recognizing someone's explanation helps to both reassure the person and move things forward, bringing a momentary closure.

Looking at the husband and wife, I asked, "Can you please tell me your side of this?"

The husband took the lead. "Well, yes, we did rent the house, but only the house." I looked at him questioningly, so he continued, "Well, there was this huge backyard garden area that we couldn't use. Every weekend he and members of his family would go through our yard and work in this big vegetable garden. They would spend the whole day there, kids and adults, using a picnic table for lunch, and the whole day they would be there. I'd hear them talking about me."

The woman was quiet while her husband spoke.

"Anyway, I'm a mechanic and I work on cars, sometimes at home in the driveway. He started to complain about it." He paused, and then continued, "We've got three kids — all boys — and they can be a little unruly at times. The neighbors called the cops on us about what they were doing.

I raised my hand. "Were police reports made?"

He nodded yes. "Yeah, there were reports. The boys were just being boys, you know, just having fun."

"What were they doing?" I asked.

A bit sheepishly, he replied, "Well, I guess they got a bit out of hand. They were shooting off their BB guns and the neighbors complained."

The plaintiff murmured, "And a lot more than that!"

I held my hand up for his silence.

The man continued, "We paid the rent on this place … have done so all along. It's not cheap, but we did it. It's got to entitle us to the use of the property. This guy doesn't seem to realize that we got rights."

Both parties had spoken now, and I knew that if any agreement were to be reached it would be in caucus, that is, in private. When parties are so dissimilar, it's difficult to accomplish agreement at the table together.

"I'd like to meet with you each separately at this point," I said. "I'd like to start with the plaintiff first." They agreed, and I led the plaintiff upstairs to the empty jury room where we could meet in a quiet corner. I started flipping through my notes and said, "I can understand how it must be difficult to go through this." Looking him in the eye, I asked, "Can you tell me about this house?"

This was just the right question to help open him up.

He explained with emotion that this was the family home and that he was from a very close-knit Greek family. He told me he was a college professor and that he had been put in charge of renting the family home. He and his brothers and sisters grew up in this house. Now they gathered every Sunday to take care of the vegetable garden, and afterwards they would go to his brother's home for dinner. This had been a lifelong ritual. Sometimes his parents would come over from their nursing facility to join them.

As I looked through the photos, it was easy to see his reason for being upset. The first picture showed a driveway with grease-stained concrete, discarded auto parts and a huge pile of rough wood. Another showed the interior of the house with tattered carpets, piles of papers and trash, a section of wall with broken plaster and a sagging door hanging heavily on a single hinge. A third image showed a bathroom with cabinet doors missing, dark cigarette burns on the countertop and a broken shower door. In all the photos, there were trash and personal items left behind. As I looked through the photos, he told me about the long list of work that was needed to return the property to a rentable condition. I was letting him run. He needed it.

Showing me a photo of the kitchen, he pointed at the stove. "You see that? That's a bullet hole in the stove! We found them all over the house. My mother cooked on that stove for thirty years! It will never be the same!"

I looked over the photos for a few more minutes with him in silence, letting him calm down after revealing his anger and grief.

Gently placing my hand on his wrist, I said, "I can understand your grief. This must be very hard for you."

He sighed and nodded.

"I should go back downstairs and talk to the other party. Are you going to be ok here?"

Dejected, he said, "Yes, I'll be ok. It's just so hard to lose your childhood home."

Going back downstairs, I rejoined the couple in the jury room. The husband looked despondent, and I guessed his wife had been talking to him.

I smiled and walked toward them. "Well, how are we doing?"

They both looked worried. "I don't want my boys in any more trouble," the man began hesitantly. I know that they shot off guns in the house, but that shouldn't make any difference in this case. The neighbors were all against us and would phone the landlord every time something wasn't to their liking." He continued speaking, his voice sounding more heated with every word. "And he was complaining about the firewood in the driveway ... why, we left him three cords of perfectly good wood! And all he had to do was to have it split, and he'd have firewood for the whole winter!"

"Yes, he showed me a picture of it," I answered. He says he will have to pay more than three hundred dollars to have it hauled off."

The room fell dead silent as the stark difference in perspectives slowly sank in.

The man thought for a moment, then continued. "Now I don't want any problems. We've moved on and can't afford to pay this bill. We've had to pay first and last on a new house, and we just don't have the money. Even if he gets the judgment, he'll have to collect it, and I'm going to string this thing out so long, he will never get his money!"

"Well, that would be for the judge to decide," I replied. He needed to fully understand what he was up against.

The woman finally spoke up. "It just don't seem fair! We paid the rent and the taxes for almost seven years and now he wants even more." I had been curious about what she would say. "I know my boys can be a little unruly at times, but they're good boys!"

I wanted to keep her talking and involved, so I led with a question. "How old are they?"

"Why, they're all teenagers now. Devon is sixteen, Eli is fourteen, almost fifteen, and Matt is twelve, almost thirteen."

Acknowledging her situation, I replied, "I would imagine they could be quite a handful."

Smiling, she insisted, "Yes, they are spirited, but I won't have them any other way." Her husband nodded, a tiny smile at the corners of his mouth.

"Still," I suggested, "you want to make sure that you can move on from this, start a new life together and leave all this behind. He has some pretty good photos of the house. He insists that there are gunshot holes in the stove and other places inside the house. He also says the neighbors were calling him during the day about gunshots and that they reported it to the police."

They both nodded and stared down dejectedly at the table. "Yeah, we heard something about that," the man muttered. "It was just a twenty-two, nothing serious."

I sensed that it was time to change the subject, always a wise course when a party feels too exposed.

"So, where did you folks move to?"

He brightened up. "We've got a great spot out in the country, a little north of Modesto. We love it. Got a few acres, got a barn for me to work in and elbow room for the boys to grow up in." She was smiling too, happy at the reminder of their new life.

"That's great!" I commented. "You've got a good place to go, and a new life to live. Now let's see how we can get you there."

"Yes," he said, truly happy and on board to establish a new life for himself and his family.

I spoke again. "Well, we better figure this thing out. I'm sure you don't want a judgment against you. I mean, the court could garnish your wages and create all kinds of havoc in your lives. I'm going to go upstairs to see if I can do something about this."

I left the table, went into the hall, and sat on the bench to take a few minutes to think things through. *What are the problems? Where are the sticking points? What would be the best solution for all the parties?* Then I had a thought ...

I went back upstairs and found the plaintiff as I had left him. He sat quietly, looking at the photos with sadness.

I walked up to him and, recognizing his intense pain, said, "This must be very hard for you. I can't imagine seeing my childhood home destroyed."

He nodded.

I continued. "I just talked with the other party, and I don't think they have any idea of what you have gone through."

He nodded again and said, "The worst part is that for the past six-plus years, every Sunday I'd go to dinner with my brothers and sisters and they blame *me* for everything that has happened." With almost a sob he continued, "They say that I haven't taken care of the family home. They look at the broken-down cars in the driveway and all the mess these people have made, and they blame *me*." The anguish in his voice was unmistakable.

This was my ah-ha moment.

I sat for a few silent moments while he gathered his thoughts. "You know, I just had an idea..." I leaned forward and took on the animated tone of a co-conspirator. "Would you mind doing something with me?"

"Sure. Why not?" he replied, intrigued.

"Okay, I'd like to work the numbers for a moment." I took out my calculator and asked, "So what was the rent that was paid every month?" He went through his notes and we added it all up. "And they paid the property taxes and other costs?"

"Yes, they were included in the rent. Since my parents have owned the house for more than forty years, they were very low."

I had his full attention.

"And the water? Including all the water you used for the garden?"

"Yes," he answered, "and the garbage, too."

Before long, we had come to a very respectable figure. The defendants had paid well over one hundred and fifty thousand dollars.

"So," I said, "I guess you now have something to tell your brothers and sisters when they say you haven't taken care of the family home." I sat back and put the tips of my fingers together in front of my chest.

He looked at the floor nodding, then he looked at me. What had started as a smile became a grin, which became a laugh as he said, "Yes!"

He grinned from ear to ear.

I raised my hand and said, "You know, we still have a hell of a mess to clean up here, but I've got an idea. Will you work with me on this?"

"Sure!" He was happy.

"I'm going back down to talk with those people. It might be a while. Are you okay here?"

"Yes," he beamed as he looked up. I could see hope on his face.

I went back downstairs to where the couple sat huddled together in the jury room. They had obviously been talking, probably about their future and how they were going to get out of this mess.

I began, "Well, I've been talking to the other side, and it's funny, you know… sometimes it's the little things that can make such a big difference. I'm not sure if you are aware of it, but the stove with the bullet hole … well, that was the stove that he grew up with so it's real important to him. I think anything that happens here will have to have an apology about that stove connected with it."

She spoke up, "I can understand that."

"Next," I said, "Do you have a pickup and a couple of buddies?"

"Why, sure I've got a pickup… got a couple of buddies that do, too," he answered.

"Well, I'm wondering what the other party would say if you offered to haul out that firewood and all the other debris that was left at the property."

The woman spoke up, "Honey, we could really use that firewood. The boys could split it, and we'd be warm all winter."

Her husband paused, making up his mind. "Well sure … I guess that would work. But we couldn't give him any money. I mean, we'd have gas and dump fees … 'course I'd have to buy the beer." Thinking more, he said aloud to himself, "There were a couple of things I left there that I could really use at the ranch."

We had the makings of a deal.

I continued back and forth between the parties, ironing out each specific issue. Finally, after a few rounds of this, both sides were content with the outcome of the mediation.

I brought the parties back together to sign the agreement in the jury room, and as I entered with the landlord-academic, the couple stood up from the table. The woman began, "We're awful sorry about what happened to the stove. We didn't know about it 'til we got home, and we did punish the boys. We took away that gun."

Thank God! I thought.

Her husband nodded in agreement.

I had not told the plaintiff that there might be an apology coming, and he was touched. Nodding and looking at the table, he mumbled a quiet, "Thank you."

We returned to the courtroom together, heads held high.

Tom, the judge, looked up, smiled, and said, "Well, I see we have another mediated agreement. You folks come right on up here. Will, we have another case for you."

And so, off to another case …

"Hello, my name is Will. Will you come this way please?"

This case settled because of the deal we were able to form where no money was exchanged. It is what I call a "performance-based" agreement. The defendants agreed to remove all the debris that they had left at the property, including the firewood. They also agreed to return three weeks later to haul away the old carpet and padding — now more than 30 years old — as well as other minor construction debris left over from the plaintiff's cleanup of the house interior. It would all be placed in the driveway for pickup. (The defendant planned to use the carpet and padding as a liner for a pond he wanted to build, but the plaintiff never knew of this reuse of the materials.) The plaintiff agreed to supply the labor and materials to refurbish the interior of the house. The defendant never knew that it would be the owner's family doing all this work.

It turned out that one of the plaintiff's family members had just lost her home to foreclosure and needed a place to live. The family could now help her.

The subdued academic would now have much to talk about at the next Sunday night dinner.

FROM THE TOOLBOX

1. The active listening technique can often lead to another powerful tool in mediation, the open-ended question:

    *   "It sounds to me that you might feel _____ about _____."
    *   "Did you mean ...?"
    *   "It seems like I'm hearing some pain in that statement. Is that true?"

2. The open-ended question can uncover how a person feels and, hence, expose their truth in the conflict.

3. Fully calculating the money involved can make a tremendous difference. Always follow the money trail. It drives so much of what we do.

4. Be creative in your thinking. All you have to do is realize what the parties want and need and help them to acknowledge it.

HEARTBREAK

There will be times as a mediator when you simply can't help someone. It comes with the territory, and you just have to take the bitter with the sweet.

This case involved two very different types of parties in terms of age, socioeconomic status and race. When dealing with someone of advanced age, it is wise to remember that the person might be suffering from some degree of dementia or the bitterness of an unfulfilled life, increasing the likelihood that they will revert to the basic defense of anger.

In a younger person intent on personal and financial growth, the emotions are very different from those of an elderly person who is more conscious of mortality and the shortness of life. When the two of these different life perspectives meet, there is frequently disagreement.

I'd come in early from a typical lunch spent in the local Safeway parking lot. It was a good day. I'd done two cases that morning, both with agreements. For that afternoon's calendar, I would be in charge of the court mediators' program because the designated program director was out of town. I was content doing what I wanted to be doing, working as a mediator and being a peacemaker.

As I walked down the hallway after passing through security, I saw Dave, the court bailiff, standing to one side of the closed courtroom doors. He was talking to a tiny African American woman — she must have weighed ninety pounds at most — who was probably seventy-plus years old with a rolling suitcase in front of her that she was banging, banging, banging against one of the doors of the courtroom. Dave was standing in front of the other door, trying to stop her from hitting either of the closed courtroom doors. Looking up at the clock in the hallway, I realized that the court was not going to open for another fifteen minutes and that Dave had probably come out of the courtroom to stop her from this loud display of frustration.

"I got rights! You get out of my way!" she loudly yelled at Dave as she banged one of the doors again with her suitcase.

Dave looked up at me plaintively. A sheriff, hearing the commotion, approached in an attempt to calm the situation. I spoke up, "Is there anything I can do to help here?"

Dave glanced at me beseechingly. "Will, we have a bit of a problem here. Do you think you can give us a hand?"

"Hello, ma'am, my name is Will. Can I be of any help to you?"

"What do you think you can do to help me?" she retorted.

"Well, why don't we sit down here on the bench? I work in this court as a mediator, and maybe I can help you."

She looked around grumpily and harrumphed an irritated assent. Dave gave me a relieved look and the sheriff went back to his station. Everyone else in the hallway backed away to give us plenty of room.

After explaining what mediation was, I said, "Ma'am, I've got to get both parties agreement to mediate this case. Are the other people here?"

She nodded and pointed down the hall. From far down the corridor, I saw a young white couple looking toward us. She glared angrily at them. "Is that the other party?" I asked.

"That's them," she answered abruptly.

"Ma'am, would you please excuse me for a moment? I've got to make sure they agree to do this."

She nodded her head in curt agreement. She wasn't happy, but it seemed I had a chance of getting her on board. *So far so good.*

I turned and walked toward the couple. Smiling, I gave my usual introduction about being a mediator for the Small Claims Court. They both looked relieved and began explaining their side of the story, that they were landlords who had had to evict her as a tenant. I held up my hand to stop them.

"Before I hear any more, we have to sign an Agreement to Mediate. Are you willing to do that?" They readily agreed.

Returning down the hall, I sat next to the woman. "Ma'am, they are willing to go to mediation if you are. We can set it up and do it after the swearing-in and roll call." I was trying to establish eye contact, but she just kept looking away. I would have to keep trying.

Dave had now unlocked the courtroom doors and announced, "Okay, folks, the courtroom is now open for anyone who has a case in this department."

As people gathered to enter, the elderly woman shoved to the front of the group, pushing her suitcase in front of her and again banging it against the door.

"Get out of my way!" she snapped as she entered the courtroom looking for a place to sit. The other people were hanging back, having seen her anger in the hallway. Dave was trying to help her, but there was no place for her and her suitcase to sit together. Looking at me, he said, "Will, how about the witness room?"

"Sure," I answered. "I'll open it up." I entered the code and opened the door. We were able to get her into the room, but we had to block the door open because she started yelling and cursing when the door closed automatically.

Dave went back into the hall. "It's all right, folks. Please come right this way."

I held one of doors open for people and ushered them in. "Please come right this way. Can you please be seated right over here?" The commotion in the hall had thrown off the standard starting procedures, and Dave and I were trying to dial the energy back down.

The other mediators had come into court also and were seated in the jury box. I joined them. We had a fire to put out together. How would we do it?

Quickly, I explained what we would do. Two mediators would go to the upstairs courtroom and handle the cases there. The two remaining mediators would handle any cases for this courtroom, and I would try to help the court with the elderly woman. They had seen the commotion in the hallway, and everyone understood immediately that this would not be the usual day in court.

I smiled inwardly. *What an honor it is to serve with these bright and capable mediators.*

Dave was going through his instruction and Jim, the court clerk, was getting ready to call the roll and swear in the disputants when I heard someone cursing loudly behind me in the witness room.

"Who the hell do they think they are, telling me what to do? These goddamn people don't know shit! I'll get 'em, get 'em good! Think they can get away with this? To hell with 'em!"

Rising, I nodded to the other mediators and to Dave and Jim, and then proceeded to the witness room.

The elderly woman was sitting in a corner, suitcase in front of her,-mumbling, "Those goddamn kids!"

Gently, I said, "Ma'am, this a court of law. You just can't talk that way here." I tried again to explain about mediation and how it might help her, ending with, "We all sign an Agreement to Mediate, and then we can talk about things. We can usually work something out."

She interrupted, "I ain't signin' nothing! And I can talk anyway I damn well please!"

Dave had come back to the witness room now as Jim was doing the roll call. "Will, we have a case for you in the other room."

"Dave, she won't sign an Agreement to Mediate. I don't think I can do much here."

"Don't worry about it. The judge will take this case first."

I returned to the courtroom. The two other mediators went out the door, escorting their parties to different locations. A quick check with them let me know where to take my group.

My case was simple, settling a business dispute through full explanations and a detailed tallying of the money involved. With the agreement signed, one party wrote a check to the other and we returned to the courtroom to have the agreement entered into the record.

There was no sign of the young couple or the elderly woman.

Sitting in the jury box was one of the other mediators, Lynn. I sat next to her and whispered, "Do you know what happened with that woman from this morning?"

She whispered, "Yes. As soon as your case is entered in the record, let's go talk in the hall."

We went out into the hall and sat on one of the benches. The hall, now quiet after the hubbub prior to the court's opening, was almost vacant.

Lynn said, "It was one of the most heartbreaking stories I've ever heard."

The woman had worked as a domestic housekeeper all her life starting at age 15. She never finished school and had married at 16. She had raised her children, and when her husband died several years ago, she lost her income from him because she was not officially married to him. The young couple had bought a house in a rapidly gentrifying area of Oakland, and the old woman lived in a basement apartment. The building was being remodeled and retrofitted, yet the woman refused to pay any rent for her unit. They tried for months to help her find a way to pay the rent, find a new place, or get some government assistance, to no avail.

In desperation, they finally called one of her children who lived in Los Angeles. He agreed to come up and help, although that's not what he did. Instead, he and his wife pulled up to the house in a moving truck, loaded everything of value into it, and drove off, leaving a mattress on the floor, some dirty blankets, and the old woman. Since they had stolen all her belongings and abandoned her, the suitcase that she was dragging around held her few remaining possessions. She was now going from shelter to shelter each night.

I hung my head as I listened to all of this, profoundly moved.

The judge had no choice but to rule for the young couple, the defendants in the case. When the elderly woman was asked by the judge how she had been able to file the case, she explained that one of the young women at the court filing counter had filled out the forms for her.

I wondered if she knew how to read and write. "I ain't signin' nothing!" rang in my ears.

The case bothered me for many weeks. I wondered what happened to her and wondered if I could have done more to help her.

In an attempt to process my emotions around this difficult case, I finally talked about it with Tim, a friend and spiritual mentor of mine for more than forty years. He suggested that I didn't and couldn't know the full story of what happened between her and her kids, and that there could have been a reason they treated her in this seemingly cruel way. Likewise, there could have been a justified reason for her anger. From the outside as mediators, we can't know everything, and we can't blame ourselves for not being able to help everyone, despite doing the best job we can.

FROM THE TOOL BOX

1. As a mediator you must not allow emotions to dictate a preference for one party over another; you must remain ever neutral and objective.

2. It is impossible for a mediator to succeed in every case. Occasional failure is, unfortunately, part of the job.

MAMA BEAR

This is a story about a young man who challenged the business practices of three major credit reporting agencies. Because credit reports are, essentially, ratings of financial responsibility, they can also determine whether a person can, say, rent an apartment or buy a house. The impact that these bureaus have on people's lives is enormous. Therefore, by working to repair his credit rating, this young man was working to protect his and his family's future.

It was the usual Friday morning for me, and I was off to court. Spring had arrived with new blossoms, new green growth showing in flowerbeds, and a crisp freshness in the air. As I walked to the courthouse, my thoughts were on the rest of year. I'd been doing this for almost two years, going in every Friday morning and working as a mediator. I'd found friends there among the staff and had been recognized as a valuable member of the court. After a lifetime spent chasing the dollar, I was finding greater fulfillment in being a peacemaker. Who would have guessed that this would happen? Not I! What would this upcoming year bring?

Passing through security, I said hello to my friend — one of the sheriffs — and loaded my belongings into the x-ray machine bin. As I was going through, there was a commotion in front of me. "Hey, that guy just stole my watch!" Immediately, one of the new sheriffs had his hand on his gun, stepping up and looking fierce. I'd seen what had happened: the watch was left in the bin.

I had to step in. "Oh, come on, guys! This is just a simple mistake. Cut it out. There's the watch." The new sheriff took his hand off the gun, the complainant took his watch, and my friend, the other sheriff, chuckled, saying, "You just can't help yourself, can you, Will?"

I smiled and nodded. Yes, he was right. I am drawn to solving conflict.

In the hallway was the usual scene of people getting ready for court. Some were going through their papers reviewing their cases, and scatterings of neatly dressed attorneys were quietly advising their clients. A few sullen faces nervously awaited their fates at the hands of justice.

I started my usual rounds — trolling for clients, as I call it. Moving from party to party, I'd try to interest people in the mediation alternative. It was simple. I'd introduce myself, find out if they were to be in that court, and make myself available to them. "Excuse me, my name is Will, and I work as a mediator in the Small Claims Court." This technique usually worked.

I approached a young man, perhaps thirty years old, dressed for court wearing a tie, sport jacket, and shined shoes. He explained to me that he was the plaintiff in the suit and that he would be willing to go to mediation. I asked him who the other party was and told him that I'd go and ask them if they were interested in mediation. He pointed to a bench across and down the hall where three people sat quietly, a man and two women, all dressed in comfortable business suits like those usually worn for traveling.

Here was an interesting group. They were obviously comfortable together. They were gathered together, each with a rolling file case for their papers, much like those many of the attorneys used. They exuded light-heartedness between them, and it was apparent they knew each other well. I approached the group smiling and introduced myself. After going through my introduction and offering mediation, they looked at each other, shrugged and said, "Sure, why not?"

I gave Dave, the bailiff, the signal as we went into court. I gave Jim, the court clerk, their names, and everything was set to move forward with the mediation process after the instruction, roll call, and swearing-in. Another mediator, Lynn, was working that morning. She really knew her stuff. I let her know that I'd gotten a case. She had too.

"How many in the party?" I asked.

"Just two. How many have you got?"

"I've got four, plus myself. I'll need the big room."

"Works for me," she said. We court mediators always worked together to try to make the mediations as comfortable as possible.

Entering the jury room, I seated the parties across from each other, signed the Agreement to Mediate, and went through my introduction, all the while trying to read the expressions of those around the table.

On one side, I've got a young man who has probably never been in a situation like this before in his life. On the other, I've got three folks who have been doing this for years and are probably a little skeptical of the mediation process. I'll have to keep the table level, I thought.

"As always, I will start with how we will address each other. My name is Will." Looking at the woman to my right, I signaled with my hand.

"My name is Connie."

The man sitting next to her chimed in. "My name is Mike."

"My name is Judy."

They all represented different credit bureaus.

I signaled the young man on my left, the plaintiff. "My name is Anthony," he replied.

I was glad we were all on a first-name basis.

"So, Anthony, what brings you to court today?"

The parties had already exchanged documents. Anthony had a slim folder of papers, which had taken the defendants maybe two minutes each to review. By contrast, the defendants each had folders about two inches thick. Anthony looked suddenly worried as he glanced through the papers inside.

He was obviously stumbling emotionally. His carefully made plans had disappeared, the rug pulled out from underneath him. He looked at me for an answer, feeling lost and alone, wondering where to start.

To get to the truth in mediation, you sometimes have to be nurturing. On one side of the table, there were three experienced people who were very good at their jobs. They looked intently at the other party who was fumbling around trying to figure out what to do.

I said, "It's okay, Son. Just tell us the truth, and we can probably figure it out."

Staring at the table, he began. "I know I screwed up." He spoke slowly and deliberately. "I was a gangbanger, out of East L.A."

A pregnant pause ensued. He had gotten everyone's attention.

"In the area that I grew up in, it was the thing to do. If you didn't, you would be in big trouble."

You could hear the truth he was telling. It came from his soul.

"I didn't know any better. I was just trying to survive," he continued.

As he told his story, I glanced over at the other side.

Their skepticism had morphed into a rapt and genuine interest in what they were hearing. Leaning closer to the table, they listened intently.

He continued, "I didn't know what else to do about this credit stuff. I wrote letters. I went through the phone numbers, talked to people and they would just refer me somewhere else. I could never talk to anyone who could do anything. I didn't know any way to talk to anyone other than to go to court."

"What did you want them to do?" I interrupted, bringing him back on point.

"Well, I wanted to talk to someone who would understand."

"Understand what?" I asked.

Plaintively he said, "That I know that I screwed up my credit rating, but I'm trying to put my life back together now."

"How are you doing that?" I asked.

Now that he was on familiar ground, he began talking faster, seemingly with more self-assuredness. "Well, I've had a job with the same company for more than five years now. I started as a laborer, and now I do concrete finishing." He continued to describe the massive transformation of his life. He had found a job and stuck with it, learned a construction trade, and become a functioning, law-abiding member of the larger society.

I listened quietly and watched the other parties. These people had undoubtedly encountered more lies and duplicity than I would hear in my entire life, but it was obvious that they realized they were hearing the young man speak honestly.

Continuing, he said, "I have a wife now and we have a baby. We're trying to move out of our one-bedroom apartment and buy a house with two bedrooms. I know we can pay for it." He dug through his slim folder pulling out pay stubs and income tax returns. The other parties nodded.

"I'm almost clear of what I did wrong. I want so much to give this to my family." He said in a failing voice.

He looked down at the table, retreating into his chair. Here was a young man who had done wrong, but then, when he had found the people that he cherished most, fought courageously for them. I looked at the three people on my right. Connie leaned back in her chair, staring pensively at the ceiling. Mike looked at the table, deep in quiet thought. Judy found a Kleenex to dab at the corners of her eyes. *Tears?*

I paused, letting the moment of quiet reflection linger.

Connie was the first one who spoke. Leaning forward, she said, "All right, let's see what we can do about this."

Thank you, Mama Bear, I thought with an inward smile, *you've found a cub.*

"Okay, I've got this in my credit report," she said, sorting through her papers and pointing out a few details. "What have you got?" she asked the others.

The three were now putting their ducks in a row.

Every incident was discussed. They were pros and were very good at their jobs — expert negotiators indeed. They went back and forth and back and forth, ironing out the details of each bump in Anthony's credit rating, clearing a new path for his financial future.

"Okay, this will fall off in six months."

"I can see he has been paying his bills, so how about we take that off now?"

"Works for me!"

"Good!"

"What about this?"

"I don't find that on my report."

"Neither do I."

"Well, it should be dropped then, okay?"

"Okay."

"Okay."

Anthony stared at the table. He had told his truth and put his future in their hands. While they hammered out the details, his look of nervous acceptance gradually gave way to a look of hopeful humility. Thirty minutes later they were done, and his new credit report would reflect the changes that had been agreed to. This would allow Anthony to move forward into his new life with his family.

We shook hands all around and shared thanks as we left the jury room. Everyone felt good about what had taken place. Anthony left with a life to look forward to, and as he walked away, Mike came up behind him, placed his hand on his shoulder, gave him a squeeze and said, "Don't worry. We all screw up once in a while."

This is exactly why I do this work, I thought.

FROM THE TOOLBOX

1. It is sometime necessary to "nurture" people, so they have the confidence to tell their truth. This is particularly true in cases where there might be socioeconomic issues, race or age factors or when the party is just plain scared.

2. When you are able to bring *truth* to the table, profound things can happen.

MESSY MAKEUP

Mediation often addresses issues that cannot be dealt with in other ways. This case involved unfortunate events that took place on an important and special day for one of the parties. Although mediation wouldn't change what happened, through mediation we crafted a creative solution that helped right the wrong that had been done. The parties reflected different personal needs, ages and different cultural and religious backgrounds. Ultimately, fulfilling the emotional needs of one side and the financial needs of the other side was what made the difference in settling the conflict.

It was the afternoon calendar, and I was fielding — like a coach with his team — the mediators. There were two different courts, more than fifty cases and four mediators plus me to work them. I had sent two mediators upstairs to the overflow court. I would remain on the first floor to put out any fires. We had become an effective part of the court system, and the judges loved it. Jim and David, the court clerks, were busy on the phone trying to anticipate the needs of the afternoon calendar.

It is amazing what happens behind the scenes in the court. The clerks set things up by running the roll call, swearing in the parties, and maintaining the court documentation. The judges and commissioners rotate between courtrooms.

After the bailiff's instructions and roll call and the clerks' swearing-in, I was asked to give an introduction to the people in the gallery about mediation as an optional process they might consider. This was a new approach; mediators had only recently become a recognized part of the court system.

I knew that another mediator was in the upstairs court, also explaining that mediation works to help solve the problems in conflict and that, because mediation was offered at no charge, most people would opt for it.

I watched as my two mediators were assigned cases while I sat in the jury gallery on the first floor. Jim signaled me over; he was on the phone with David upstairs. Covering the mouthpiece, he whispered, "Will, they need you upstairs." I nodded and headed up.

As I entered the upstairs court, the judge summoned me to the bench. "We have a case here that I believe needs a mediator. The two here are already assigned to cases. Will you take this one?"

"Of course, Your Honor."

I motioned to the litigants. "Will the parties please join me?"

As I held the doors open to leave the courtroom, they came toward the rear of the room.

One side consisted of an attractive young couple, both around twenty years old, dressed neatly for court, appearing to be of middle-eastern origin and looking a little angry. The other party was a somewhat portly, older middle-eastern man wearing slacks and opened-neck shirt, also looking angry.

Oh boy, I thought. *Here we go.*

We joined the other mediations going on in the jury candidates' waiting room on the third floor and found a quiet corner. I did my introduction, and we signed the documents that would cover us under the California laws regarding confidentiality. The couple were the plaintiffs and they were asking for the maximum claim. The older gentleman was the defendant.

After going through my introduction and the document exchange, I turned to the plaintiffs first. "Thank you for doing this mediation and giving this process a try. It would help me understand your case if you can tell me in your own words what has brought you to court today."

The young man took the lead. "Well, we're here today to get what we rightfully paid for."

Calmly, I asked, "And this case is about…?"

He continued a little more slowly. "We hired this individual to do all the coordination of our wedding and he did a terrible job." His wife was looking wistfully away as he talked. "His company was paid to provide us with all the things necessary for our wedding. All the catering, the limousine, the photographs … everything we wanted."

Still looking away, a pained expression spread across his wife's face as she remembered the event.

I asked, "What went wrong?" I turned toward the husband and gave him my full attention as he jumped into his side of the story.

"We are from Pakistan … that is to say, our parents are from Pakistan. We were born and raised in this country. Our wedding was of great importance to us, and the photos of it were also of the greatest importance. My grandmother could not attend, nor could my wife's grandparents, nor the rest of our family who are over there. We were assured that the photos we would get would cover the whole ceremony and reception, so we could mail photo discs to our family in Pakistan. But the photos we got were very bad and incomplete. We know they took more of them because we were in them!"

I could tell he was starting to feel at ease because he had found an audience. Active listening is one of the strongest tools a mediator can use to help get to the heart of a conflict. The wife was still looking away forlornly as she remembered how her important day had been ruined.

The other party had been reviewing his notes this entire time, seemingly indifferent, offering no eye contact, his thoughts sealed within himself.

The young man continued with emotional force. "The quality of the disc that we got was terrible! The pictures were out of focus, there were almost no photos of the guests, and only two formal shots of the wedding party. I *know* they took more. We were there for half an hour! He ruined our wedding!" The wife nodded sadly.

I slowly nodded, letting him know that I had heard his side of the argument and his pain.

I asked, "Can we hear from the other side now?"

The young man responded with a curt "Yes."

"Please sir, could you tell us your side of this?" I used my best persuasive tone.

He began, "I really don't see what they are complaining about. I was the contractor for their wedding, and I fulfilled my contract, and they still owe me several hundred dollars. The photographer was a subcontractor. They should be suing him, not me."

I held up my hand, "Excuse me, but were you the prime contractor?"

"Yes. It's my business to do traditional weddings for people that want them." He continued," These people requested a traditional wedding, and I furnished them with it." He ruffled through his papers. "Here you can see the contract they signed. It specifies that they chose the photo packet that only had thirty pictures." He ended by looking at the young man.

Okay, let's see if we can first get them talking, I thought.

I signaled the young man to respond.

"Yes, that's true, but we were supposed to be able to choose which ones. We never even got to see them all!"

"That's not my fault. The photographer was a subcontractor," he replied.

Both parties were now quiet.

Oh well. That didn't work so well, I thought. *Onward.*

I went into a reflective summation of what I thought I had heard. "As I understand it, this situation was brought about by, in part, the lack of photos that were necessary to be sent back to the families." I went on, mentioning everything they had said, getting a nod from each side as I spoke.

I was at least getting them to agree about where they were and what they had said.

"I feel that I know so much more about what has happened. Thank you for telling me."

I sat back in my chair and relaxed, which allowed them to do likewise, and then asked, "Would either of you mind if we caucused? I've got a couple of questions that I would like to ask you separately. The caucus will be confidential."

All agreed, and I asked the defendant if he would mind going into the hall to wait.

After he had gone, I addressed the wife first because she had not spoken at all. "I can't imagine how hard this must have been for you, your very special day ruined."

The floodgates opened.

"It was just terrible! After the ceremony, we drove to the reception hall. Everyone was there, but we had to sit in the limo until the photographer got there and he was over two hours late! We kept trying to get him" — she motioned with a sideways nod at the plaintiff's seat — "on the phone, but he wouldn't answer. Everyone was waiting, and the food was getting cold. I was so upset and unhappy, and it was so hot in the limo, parked in the sun."

The husband chimed in. "Yeah, and the makeup was running down our faces." He traced his fingertips down his face. "The limo driver wouldn't even turn on the air conditioning because he didn't want to use up the gas."

Ah, I thought. *a piece of the puzzle.*

She continued, and while crying softly said, "And all of our guests were just waiting for us, for over two hours! We were stuck in the car, the makeup running down our faces, and we couldn't do anything!"

I let her sit in silence for a couple of minutes as her husband stroked her back soothingly.

Good lad, I thought, smiling inwardly.

I acknowledged their pain saying, "I'm very sorry that this has happened to you."

"Well, after the photographer finally showed up, we had the pictures taken. There were more than two hundred guests, and some of them had already started on the food, so we seated everyone as fast as we could and had our meal. It had gotten so late, and we were so tired that we didn't even go over to the hotel for our honeymoon night. We just went home."

She looked despondent. Who could blame her?

I asked, "You didn't even get your honeymoon night out together?"

She just shook her head no.

"Thank you for sharing this with me. I'm going out in the hall to talk to the other party. Please be comfortable here until I return."

The wedding coordinator was standing out in the hall talking on his cell phone. He held up his hand as I approached, signaling that he needed more time.

I waited while he finished the call.

Sitting down on the bench, I signaled him to sit beside me.

"Well, after hearing their side, I'm really interested in hearing yours." I continued, "I understand that you are a wedding planner and, as you have said, you do traditional weddings for several different faiths. I really don't know much about that business. Could you tell me something about it?"

On familiar ground, he began his story. "Yes, that's the business I have. I've been doing it for many years, and it's a successful business." He then went into detail about all the different kinds of traditional faith weddings his company coordinated. As he was talking, he became more of a businessman describing the different things that were necessary to do his work successfully. He spoke comfortably and with pride.

Good! I thought. I was getting him to talk and be involved.

He spoke for perhaps ten minutes before I asked my first question. "So, I guess one problem here is the photos?"

"Yes," he replied. "The photographer is a subcontractor in my business. He is the one to blame here, not me. He should have been the one to be sued, not me."

I continued, "I guess the market must be small for these kinds of weddings?"

"Yes," he agreed. "But we're very good at this."

"I'd also guess that it's pretty much a word-of-mouth business?"

"Yes."

"Forgive me, but I have to ask this question. What do you think this couple will say to others? You know … what they might post about what happened to them?"

I continued, "I'd guess that most of your clients are younger. That's the same group that goes online to get information, and an unfavorable comment or comments might have some impact. I'm just here to help you think about things so you can make a good decision, but what do you think?"

This was his "ah-ha" moment.

"I hadn't thought of that," he said slowly. He had been so invested in being right and defending himself that he had lost his perspective of the larger issues that might affect his business.

"Maybe I should just let you think about things for a couple of minutes," I said. "Could you do me a favor? Could you find out if the photographer still has any of the photos he took, you know, just in case?"

He reached for his phone, and you could tell he was thinking about things he hadn't considered before.

Returning to the jury room, I found the couple sitting close together, hunched over looking dejected.

Approaching them, I said, "I can't image what it must have been like," mimicking the young man's movements, running my fingertips

59

down my face, "the makeup running into your eyes and down your face." They looked at me and smiled, paused, looked at each other, chuckled, and then burst out laughing. "Yes!" they both said. "Yes! That was just what it was like!"

I sensed some of their anger release with my gesture.

"I couldn't *believe* it … all the planning, all the money we spent," he exclaimed. "This guy cheated us. And the photos just sucked!"

I let them enjoy the moment as they shifted from despair to laughter.

By mimicking them, did I offer an insight into how they looked and felt at the wedding, I wondered? And now they were in the here-and-now. Did my recognition of their feelings allow them to transition from pain and resentment to acceptance? I didn't know, but this technique seemed to work.

After a couple of minutes, we returned to the case, laughing. "Okay," I said, "We have to move forward with this. It seems like what bothered you most was not being able to send the photos home, the messy makeup, the fact that everything didn't go as it should and that you felt you didn't get what you paid for."

They both agreed. "Okay, I'm going to go back and talk to the other party. Is there anything that we've talked about that I can't share with him?"

After looking at each other with questioning looks, then back at me, they said, "No."

I went back into the hall, and the wedding planner was on the phone again, but he hung it up as soon as he saw me.

This time he started the conversation. "I just talked to the photographer, and he still has the pictures, about two hundred of them on disc."

I responded, "Well, that's a relief. It would have really been a shame if the only pictures were the ones those kids have."

We both sat down as I continued, "I've been talking with them about the things that bothered them about the way the wedding coordination went. One of the issues they mentioned was that when they were in the limo, they kept trying to phone you, but you never answered."

Looking away, he answered, "I was in India. I got called home to my family and had to go."

"Oh, that would explain it!" I said.

"What happened to the photographer?" I continued. "Why was he more than two hours late?"

"Well, he's a subcontractor. In my business I have the photographer work directly with the clients as to what photos they want and how many. It's up to him to get paid for the work. I just take a percentage." Looking at the floor, he said, "I didn't know it, but he took another job on that day. It was only supposed to take half an hour, but there were problems, so it took more than two hours for that shoot."

Another piece of the puzzle, I thought.

"So, the photographer should take some of the blame?"

"Oh yes! I just got off the phone with him, and he knows how I feel about this!"

"Will he give up the disc?"

"Yes, at no charge." We were making progress.

"Well, I'm not sure if you know about this, but I asked those kids about what happened while they were stuck in the limo." I then told him the tale about the limo being parked in the sun with their makeup running down their faces, and the driver refusing to turn on the air conditioning, for more than two hours. I told him how some two hundred friends and family waited and then began to eat the reception meal without the bride and groom being present, adding that the couple had had to cancel their honeymoon night in San Francisco.

He nodded and looked at the floor while I talked.

Sighing, he said, "Yes, I understand."

"So, what do you think should happen here? I mean, we have

the chance to make things as right as we can at this point in time." I then gave a summation of all that I saw involved in the situation.

Then I did some risk assessment, helping him to evaluate potential dangers that this conflict might hold for him.

"They've withheld the money for the photographer ... a few hundred dollars. You don't want them bad-mouthing you. What is that worth? We don't know what the judge will say, but you were the prime contractor on this job and are responsible for it with a contract signed by both parties. What do you think?"

He was looking at the deep waters of potential reputation damage and income loss. He didn't want negative comments about his business posted online or shared in the community. He needed a way out, so I threw him a life preserver.

"Okay, suppose you offer them all the photos at no charge. It's no money on your part. The photographer has already agreed to give them the disc at no charge. Let's also suppose that to protect your reputation, we ask them to agree to say nothing derogatory about you on any website or in the community. They could only say that there were problems, but that they were worked out to their satisfaction. What do you think?"

He nodded and looked hopeful.

"Let's also say that you make some sort of contribution to them so that they might have a wedding night out. You know, the young lady hasn't said much, but I think it might really help them move forward from this conflict and help her launch their marriage in a positive way like they had planned. What do you think?"

"Yes, I'll give them two hundred dollars."

It was time to strike a full deal.

I went back to the young couple. They sat in a sunny corner of the jury gathering room, smiling and looking up at me. I felt welcomed.

Sitting down with them, I said, "I think we have the initial makings of a deal here. First, I think we can get a copy of all the photos so that you can send the disc to your family." This was the most important thing for them and their family, pictures of the start of their future life together.

"But there are a few things that will have to happen to make this deal go through." They listened attentively. "First, you have to agree not to make derogatory comments about what has happened. You might just say that, although there were things that happened that were bad, in the end it all turned out okay." They both nodded. "Next, let's address the payment that you've withheld for the photographer. He has now agreed to give you a clean copy of the disc at no charge to you. I understand that there are more than two hundred photos." They readily agreed. "Finally," looking at the young woman, I said, "I noticed that you didn't have your honeymoon night out." She glumly nodded. "I have talked to him about this, and he thinks that you should have that night out so that your marriage is launched correctly." She was flabbergasted. She had been quiet about the importance of this, perhaps embarrassed by her own need, but it had been obvious to me. "He has made an offer of two hundred dollars to try to correct this. Will that be enough?"

They had gotten what they wanted most: the photos. I could see that understanding the full outcome and shifting from despair to joy would take a few more minutes to sink in.

I gently held up my hand and said, "Please just think about this. I'm going to talk to the other party."

By leaving them for a few moments, I gave them time to process their plans and emotions.

The wedding planner was now sitting down on the bench. Walking up to him I said, "We almost have a deal. The only sticking point is the night out. They had planned to go to a very nice hotel and with the dinner, the room and everything ... it might be more than two hundred dollars."

He spoke up immediately, "Okay, I'll go up to three hundred dollars ... but that's my final offer."

"Okay, I'll take that back to them."

I returned to the young couple. They were now sitting back happily, relaxed and smiling.

Before they could say anything, I said, "Well, he really wants you kids to start off right. He thinks that three hundred dollars would be a better number to make sure of that."

The young man was looking down, nodding his head affirmatively. His wife stood up and hugged me, tears in her eyes, saying, "Thank you."

I wrote up the agreement, noting privately that both sides got what they needed to move on. Bringing the wedding planner back into the jury room to sign the document, the two parties addressed each other very differently.

The wedding planner said, "I'm so sorry about what happened."

The young man responded, "Thank you for saying that and for your generosity with us." With tears in her eyes, the young lady grasped the wedding planner's hand and nodded her head in gratitude saying, "Thank you." The wedding planner looked at me and nodded his head in gratitude.

I felt paid in full. There are some things that money can't buy.

After shaking hands, all of us smiling, I led them back to the courtroom.

In this court, I always took my paperwork up to Art, the bailiff. He gave me a soft, acknowledging fist bump. David, the court clerk, looked up at me. "Another one, Will?"

I nodded.

Art went to get the judge.

David motioned me over to kneel down beside him. Whispering, he said, "Will, what the hell are you doing out there? The clerks are keeping track, and you're at ninety-eight percent resolution rate while all the other mediators are about fifty to sixty percent."

Wow, they're keeping track, I thought. *I wonder if there's a pool going on me ...*

I answered honestly, "David, I just listen to them. They know what they need out of this. I just listen and help them find solutions to the problems that will meet their needs."

As the judge entered the courtroom, David announced, "This court is now in session,"

The judge read over the agreement, confirmed that both parties were in accord with it, and entered it into the record. Leaving the bench, he looked at me intently with burning curiosity. As the parties shook hands a final time as they left the courtroom, the wedding planner, smiling, held the door open for the young couple.

In this case, the acknowledgment of personal pain and emotion of one party was a crucial first step in reaching an agreement.

Feeling understood helped them shift from their previous stance to a new understanding of past events. There is an old expression in the psychological community, "Pain shared is pain halved." This is also true in mediation.

FROM THE TOOL BOX

1. The caucus allowed the parties to express themselves without fear of re-igniting or escalating the conflict.

2. Empathically mimicking the physical expression of the plaintiffs brought recognition of their shared experience. In this case it allowed laughter and the release of past events.

3. The evaluative technique of risk assessment helped one of the parties better understand the risk his position could expose him to, thus helping him make a more informed decision about possible outcomes.

SABOTEUR

Some cases don't settle through mediation. The reasons can be many and varied. In this case, a person who was not named in the lawsuit but who attended the mediation conference had a personal agenda for sabotaging the proceedings. I had to put my foot down to avert impending chaos. The most important rule is that a mediator cannot lose control of the table.

It was a rainy Friday morning, cold and wet with the sharp bite of winter, and those waiting in line to enter court had to stand in the icy rain. No one was happy. I was under my umbrella midway in this line stretching for more than a block when I noticed two women several groups in front of me, who were acting strangely.

It's interesting what you can learn about people by just watching them when they are forced to stand in the rain. One of the two women, all in black, kept turning around and glaring back fiercely toward the end of the line, shooting hateful looks at a man standing there. The anger and resentment showed clearly in her eyes.

I couldn't help but look over my shoulder to see whom she was looking at. The man she was targeting appeared just as antagonistic as he shot piercing looks in return and made sidelong comments to his companion as they stood under their black umbrellas. These two men were both dressed Friday-casual in raincoats, sports jackets and open shirts. Turning back toward the two women in front of me, I tried to figure out what was going on. The other woman was blonde, in her mid-thirties, slightly overweight and dressed in a loud, bright pink, floral, free-flowing blouse, white tight-fitting pants, pink flat style shoes and a light pink rain jacket — an ensemble that felt a tad garish for court. The other woman wore all black: a black leather jacket, black Levi's, black shirt and shoes. Even her shortly cropped hair was dyed black. It was apparent by the women's interactions that they were a couple. The one in black was trying to shelter her partner with her jacket from the rain and seemed to be trying to reassure her verbally. Peering over my shoulder again to the man who received the chilling looks from the woman dressed in black, I could see that the man had now defiantly turned his back to her. The line snaked slowly forward and as soon as the women made it under an eave before the doors, the one in black turned and again sneered nastily at the guys behind me, seemingly glad the men would have to endure a longer wait in the cold rain.

Oh boy, that's going to be a tough case! I thought to myself.

I never dreamed that I would be involved.

People filed into the courtroom as I strode down the hall, shedding my raincoat and hat, folding up my umbrella, and entering the jury box where the mediators sit.

Dave, the bailiff, started his spiel. "Okay folks, here is what we're going to do." He used casual language for maximum effect. As he talked, I looked over the gallery. It was about half full, with a random hodgepodge of people from all walks of life, and there, seated as far apart as possible, were the people I had watched in line.

As luck would have it, I was the only mediator that morning. *Oh boy*. I thought, I'd have my hands full.

My first case turned out to be a pretty easy one involving two men who had been in business together. Their beef was about who was responsible for the debts that were left after terminating their co-owned business. After using the standard tools — letting each party tell his truth (emotional parts included), reflective conversation about what I'd heard and having each listen to the other — the turning point was reached. Both realized the loss they felt at the failure of the enterprise and realized that neither one was at fault. Each one kindly volunteered to pay for things in the original disagreement. The feeling of tension and anger was now gone, both men forgiving the other and themselves for what had happened. The friendship they had shared, which included dinners, vacations and time spent together, could now be renewed with greater understanding, if only through the recognition of how important their friendship was to each of them. They could move forward with their lives.

This is the best kind of outcome and this is why I do this work: to create better understanding and forgiveness so people can figure a way out of conflict. Finally, with the mediated agreement in hand they stood, shook hands, and apologized to each other.

I smiled inside.

We returned to the courtroom and I handed the documents to Jim, the court clerk. Tom, our judge, looked over and said, "Well, I see that we have another mediated agreement. Is there anyone else who is willing to go to mediation?"

I always had great respect for Tom. Being a judge can make someone sealed off and uncompassionate, yet Tom consistently displayed the opposite of that, unless of course someone disrespected the Court.

Then he focused on the people I'd seen in the line, "We have a mediator here who has a fantastic success rate."

I quailed inside, wondering if his statement might suddenly enact Murphy's Law and signal the beginning of the end of my winning streak.

"I hate to see a mediator who is not working. How about trying mediation?"

Coming from the bench, it's a no-choice issue. They all nodded, and I got the case.

As I walked past Dave, he whispered a warning, "Watch it, Will. This guy's an asshole."

Yeah, Dave, I've got a feeling there's more than one here, I thought wryly.

Leading them from the courtroom to the adjacent jury room, I was as gracious as I could be, holding the door open, kindly leading with expressive hand movements. "Please come in. Please be seated here. Please get comfortable." All the while I was trying to decompress their excessively high tension. For the most part, they were civil. Sitting across from each other, they got their paperwork together — lots of material from the men and a minimal amount from the women.

After signing an Agreement to Mediate, I started with my rap. "Has anyone here been through mediation before?" The man Dave had warned me about spoke up first. "Why, yes, I've been in mediation before. As a landlord I've had to deal with plenty of deadbeat tenants who don't pay their rent."

It was not starting out positively. I raised my hand, "I will not allow any disrespect to take place at this table."

This is going to be a tough one, I thought.

Looking at the blonde defendant, I asked, "Have you been in mediation before?"

"No, I have never been in anything like this before."

Glancing at the woman in black, I just inquired with my eyes trying to establish contact.

"I'm just here to help my friend. This guy is just trying to get her," she said, leaning back smugly in her chair. She remained closed and vigilant.

Gently holding up my hand again, I launched further into my introduction. "Mediation is a confidential process where people are allowed via California laws to talk honestly about their conflict."

As usual when I'm going through this part of the process, I looked around the table, establishing eye contact with each person and trying to dial down and de-escalate the energy by using a calm tone of voice and expressive gentle hand movements. It seemed to be working. It usually does.

Continuing, I explained my ground rules, making sure everyone understood how we would proceed. I asked the plaintiff to start the process.

He started in immediately. "I've got an apartment complex in Hayward, and I rented to the defendant. She was there for nineteen months after signing a two-year lease." As he was talking, he was laying out paperwork on the table all in order; he had done this before. "This is my property manager," signaling to the man sitting next to him. "He can testify as to all the property damage that had to be repaired, as well as to the broken lease."

I let him speak for a few more minutes while he told of late payments and how he had "bent over backwards" to help the tenant, as well as how he had been used by her. She moved out still owing back rent, and the apartment needed extensive repairs to return it to rentable condition. In addition, there was some time that he was unable to rent the apartment due to the needed repairs. His figures showed that the defendant owed several thousand dollars beyond the security deposit that had not been returned.

I then signaled the defendant to speak.

She looked overwhelmed but was trying to address the problem. "Yes, I did rent the apartment with my previous partner. It was the only way I could afford to do it. We were together for about one year, and then we broke up and I could no longer pay the rent."

I asked, "Did the partner sign the lease also?"

"No, she didn't sign the lease."

"Please go on." I was speaking softly, trying to help her get her story out by intently listening.

"I tried to talk to him about it. I tried to explain, but he just wouldn't listen. He just kept going on about the rent and the lease, and I didn't know what to do."

I was trying to be supportive and understanding, giving her

time to tell her story. Glancing over at the men, I saw that they were looking away, uninterested.

As she went on, she told of the breakup with her partner and the impact it had had on her life, and how she had been cut back in her hours on her job because of the time she took off to deal with her emotional turmoil. She spoke in detail of how much she had loved that person and the trauma of losing her. She was honestly telling her emotional story of pain and the loss of her previous lover. Perhaps that's why the next events unfolded.

After she seemed to be finished, I gave a reflective statement about what I'd understood from each party. In this process, I go back and forth between the parties establishing the common points that both agree on, for example, rental start date, rents paid and still owed, the final condition of the apartment, staying away from discussing the "lost love" aspect. While doing this, I noticed the woman in black was just sitting back in her chair, away from the table, looking very unhappy and angry.

Remembering them together in the rain, the hateful glances by the defendant's new partner toward the landlord and her apparent protectiveness, I wondered, *is she perhaps jealous?* Her anger was plain to see.

The reflective-statement technique can often start the agreement process, but not this time. The landlord started talking about how the defendant's credit rating would suffer if he got a judgment against her and how she would never be able to rent an apartment until she paid him what she owed him.

Then the woman in black spoke up angrily. "That doesn't matter. She lives with *me* now!"

I intervened by reminding them, "I believe that we are all trying to reach an agreement here that will be of benefit to all of you."

The woman in black leaned forward, toward the landlord across the table and smiled. "I'm not interested in a mediated agreement.

I'm just here to tell this son of a bitch what I think of him," she said, looking him in the eye.

Immediately I said, "Now wait, that's not going to work here." But I was ignored, and the woman in black and the landlord started arguing, each loudly saying what they thought of each other, completely ignoring the mediation rules of no insults or profanity.

Half rising out of my chair, I raised my voice above theirs. "This will stop now!" Again, I was ignored, and now the other two started in. Within 30 seconds the mediation had blown apart.

Finally rising to my full 6'4" height, I slammed my hand down flat on the table between them as hard as I could. "WHERE THE HELL DO YOU THINK YOU ARE?"

Instantly I had four wide-eyed quiet chipmunks, sitting in their chairs with paws up, frightened deer-in-the-headlights looks, frozen in place.

"This is a court of law, and if you think that kind of behavior is going to work here, you are wrong! If you think either I or the judge or anyone else here is going to put up with this, you are wrong!"

As I was gathering up my papers to leave, I continued. "This is not some kind of grudge fest where you can just do whatever you please, say whatever you want. No matter what you think, the judge will decide what happens today according to the law. Frankly I'm finished here."

We returned to the courtroom. As we were leaving, the landlord, who was the last one out of the room, said to me, with eyes still wide, "That was *goood.*"

I'm sure that my loud statement had been overheard in the courtroom, but nothing was ever said. Indeed, everyone in the entire courtroom just smiled at me as I walked back in.

In this case, the judge ruled in favor of the landlord for most of the amount requested. When one of the parties expressed the love and pain of her failed relationship, the insecurity of the new partner was exposed. The judgment that was given by the court insured that the defendant's credit rating was destroyed and her ability to rent again was completely compromised. This provided security for the new partner. She had a vested interest in not having a mediated agreement, because it would have diminished her power in their personal and financial relationship.

FROM THE TOOL BOX

1. A mediator must maintain control of the table. In this case I could see there was no hope of an agreement and so I took control and ended the mediation proceedings.

2. It is important to remember that all the players at the table have a stake in the outcome, and most people will foster their own interests above anyone else's.

3. The use of gracious conduct by the mediator, gentle hand and voice movements, and eye contact effectively facilitate the possibility of a compromised agreement. Such gestures will at least allow the parties to sit down together.

PUPPY LOVE

This case involved transitional moments of emotion in which I, as the mediator, had to be attuned to all parties' feelings. Compassion on my part was most important to allow the parties to connect fully.

It was another Friday morning and I was headed to court. I looked forward to Fridays more than any other day of the week because I could see my courthouse friends and take part in my most enjoyable and fulfilling work — helping people solve intractable conflict.

My first case that morning involved a young couple. They were both white, in their early twenties, and betrayed extreme nervousness by their darting glances. They were there to settle bills related to having lived together before an emotional breakup.

I'd done quite a few of these cases and they were generally a simple matter of arithmetic to divide the financial responsibility appropriately. The emotions, however, could be a real bear, especially in a case like this one involving a recent breakup.

Holding the jury room door open for them, I motioned to chairs across from each other, seating myself at the head of the table. I took my tablet, calculator and file of court forms out of my briefcase.

"Thank you for agreeing to take part in this process. In mediation, there exists the chance for you to understand each other better and to work through the problems that brought you here. You know the problems far better than I ever will, and you also know your own needs." Pausing, I added, "I am here to help facilitate that discussion."

They both nodded their heads, neither establishing eye contact with the other.

I continued my introduction, sizing up the emotions I was sensing from them.

The young woman, the defendant, sat stiffly in her chair, arms clenched at her sides, staring directly in front of her. She trembled with nervous tension.

What has happened here? I wondered. She seemed so fragile.

The young man, Randy, slouched back in his chair. He tried to find a comfortable position but fidgeted continuously, leaning forward to restack the papers on the table in front of him, then leaning back again in nervous agitation.

After my introduction and the paperwork exchange, we started with the plaintiff's statement.

"I didn't know how else to get a hold of you," Randy stated meekly.

I held up my hand. "What is this case about?" It's important to start at the basics.

He started over. "Suzie and I used to live together, and I have all these bills that she left me with. I'm here to get the money to pay them off."

"I don't have any money," she replied softly.

I once again raised my hand and said gently, "If we are going to be able to do this, please don't interrupt."

"Do you have a listing of the bills?"

"Yes, they are in the file that she just looked through."

"Is there anything else you want to tell us?" I asked.

"I still love you, Suzie," Randy began. And then the dam broke.

With a breaking voice and a gentle sob, he cried as he told of how much he missed her, of how he wished that what had happened had not happened.

She was now gently sobbing, too.

I passed out some of the packets of tissues that I always keep on hand. If you are doing this kind of work, you will definitely need them sooner or later.

I knew we needed to take this case slowly to let the emotions sink in, so I let them compose themselves while we all sat quietly together. I then asked Suzie if she would like to say anything.

Nodding her head slowly, looking at the table she started to speak.

"Randy, it's just not going to work out. I can't live the way you want to." She then told her side of the story, speaking of the chaotic life they had lived together. She was very forthcoming and honest, both about what worked and, more importantly, what didn't: the constant party atmosphere, the drug and alcohol use, the feeling of never feeling safe or knowing what would happen next.

Finally, she said, "Randy, I'm sure that the reason you got so violent that night was because you'd been drinking and doing all those drugs."

A good thing was happening here. The truth that each one needed to hear was coming forth. I decided to just keep them talking.

Randy nodded his head in sad agreement, looking at the floor.

She went on, "I was so scared. You were driving behind me, and I couldn't get away from you. You were driving crazy! And then when you were arrested, I decided then and there that I just couldn't do it anymore."

Randy, still staring at the floor, nodded.

We all sat quietly for perhaps five minutes, letting the moments pass while each of them reflected on the past events. They had calmed down, both now seeming more relaxed, and they started to establish eye contact.

I wanted to give them plenty of time, but also knew I needed to help them move forward.

I finally breeched the silence, speaking softly and calmly. "I can certainly understand how this must be very painful for you both. It's not always easy when people find themselves in this kind of situation.

In fact, it's probably one of the hardest things we can face in life." I acknowledged their pain and paused to let it sink in.

"In my life there have been times when someone I cared a great deal for has broken it off. It's very rough. For what it's worth, I've found three things I say to myself that help. One, no matter how good or bad things are, they will change. Two, tomorrow is another day. And three, I need to keep moving forward because, by doing so, I change my options."

They pondered these words for a few moments. Then they both looked up and smiled for the first time.

Randy suddenly replied, "I really didn't want to make you pay for all this stuff. It was just a way to get you to talk to me."

Suzie looked intently at him for the first time and said, "I understand. We should have had this talk a long time ago."

I leaned back in my chair and moved back from the table, listening to them talk. Healing was taking place.

Looking at each other, they had a very poignant talk. They began to speak with an emotional depth that included both love and pain. There were smiles in some places, shaking voices in others, and the softness of sorrow in their words. They each apologized to the other and accepted the past events with a release.

I let them talk for almost fifteen minutes, and when their pauses grew longer I moved back to the table and said gently, "We are going to have to do something about this case."

Suzie said, "Just one more thing." Looking quizzically at Randy she asked, "How's Rex?"

"Rex?" I asked.

Randy answered, "Rex is our dog. He misses you, Suzie."

"I miss him so much." Suzie said. "Will I ever be able to see him again?"

I looked at Randy, he looked at Suzie, and we came to an agreement. The deal was simple. Randy would not enforce any action against Suzie for the bills. Suzie would not speak badly about Randy, and at some time in the future after she had started her new life, she would give him a payment for the bills. Randy would not bother her in any way. Rex would be shared by them, the arrangements for which would be made through a mutual friend.

Dog visitation rights. That was a first for me.

Mediation often provides the chance for people to speak honestly about what is really bothering them. After going through the initial stages of emotional release of tension and anxiety, there exists the chance to go deeper into the conflict.

There are mediators who would not agree with adding any personal advice. My advice did, however, provide both parties with a stepping-stone out of their conflict so they could find both recognition and forgiveness.

FROM THE TOOL BOX

1. Find common positive ground to establish a shared connection between the parties involved. In doing so, you can help them make the transition from conflict to hope of change.

2. Maintain control of the table by monitoring the emotional issues in a constructive way as they come forth. I think of it as having a control valve, closing when I hear insults or antagonism, opening when the parties are having a constructive dialogue.

3. Give the parties the time they need to assimilate the information and respond to it when they are having a constructive dialogue.

STICKY POINTS

Mediators use the term "sticky points" to describe areas of congestion or blockage in the mediation process. These points frequently center on charged emotions of anger, pain, or need — emotions that may ultimately be the driving force behind a person's investment in the conflict itself. When parties reveal, acknowledge and explore these sticky points, it can result in their personal transformation, which can then lead to effective conflict resolution.

It was a Friday morning in December. I woke at 7 a.m., showered, shaved, and dressed in my court get-up of a jacket and slacks and no tie. The courtroom staff all wore ties; I tried to look different but still like a member of the court. I arrived at the courthouse and went through the usual court routine: lining up outside, waiting to go through security, saying hello to the sheriffs and seeing if anyone in the hallway was interested in mediation. Entering the courtroom, I greeted the staff of the court whom I regarded as friends. While these folks are usually considered to be on the sidelines, they actually run the courtrooms. The commissioners and judges often rotate between courts and are not present on a daily basis. I had checked the court calendar posted in the hallway outside and saw that there were not many cases that morning, probably because it was the holiday season, a time when most folks prefer not to be dealing with the arduous grunt work of legal cases.

Every year people would file for their cases to be heard either just before or just after the winter holidays. The court calendars were therefore small in early December.

Juan, a newly minted mediator, was working with me that morning. Because I had done so much work over the past two years, I decided to give him the morning's one contested case where both parties had come to court. Often there were cases where only one party was present. If both parties had been served and only one appeared, the plaintiff, who was usually the one to show up, would get a favorable decision.

Juan would probably welcome an interesting case, I reasoned. I would have a chance to work in the afternoon's large calendar and would probably have cases to do then.

We went through the standard check-in process: roll call, swearing-in by the court clerk and instruction to the gallery by Dave, the bailiff, who then asked if anyone would be willing to go to mediation. The parties in the one contested case volunteered and I signaled to Juan to take the case. I stayed in the jury box.

About five minutes after Juan had taken the case to the jury room behind me, I heard a woman's loud shriek through the jury room door.

"You fucking bitch! I'll kill you!"

I looked at Tom, the judge, and he looked at me as I said, "Excuse me, your Honor," already heading out of the courtroom doors as fast as I could.

In the hall I found an African American woman fleeing the jury room. She was in her mid-30's, dressed for court and wide-eyed with shock.

I asked, "Wow, are you okay?"

At this she exhaled. "Yeah. I'll be okay. It's just that that woman is such a BITCH!"

"Okay, can we just sit for a couple of minutes in the hall?" I had a fire going here, so I was trying to absorb the flames.

"Yes. Thank you." She took a deep breath.

We sat in the now empty corridor hall and waited a few moments. I was trying to help her tension drain away by exhibiting calmness myself. After both of us had decompressed, releasing the tension of what had just happened, I asked her to explain.

She started to tell me her case, giving a brief outline of the events. I nodded with understanding as I listened. I then explained that I had not signed the Agreement to Mediate form and so was not yet covered under the law to mediate her case.

"I understand that you volunteered for mediation and I want to help you do that. Would you be willing to stay here for a couple of minutes while I go and get signed in? Are you still willing to mediate this case?"

She nodded in firm agreement.

Going back into the jury room, I found Juan and the other party still seated at the table. On one side sat a well-dressed middle-eastern man and woman with their heads bent in conference.

Juan looked up at me almost plaintively and said, "I don't know what happened, Will. It just all came apart at once. I tried to do the intro, and they just started at it and wouldn't listen to me."

The couple was sitting with their heads down, their papers spread out in front of them.

"Emma, why did you do that?" the man asked. "We talked about this and agreed about how we were going to do this."

"Excuse me for interrupting," I said, "but I have not signed the Agreement to Mediate document. If you are willing to continue this mediation with my help, I have to sign it so that I am covered under California law and to protect myself from suit."

Juan looked at the couple, they nodded their consent, and he slid the form over to me, which I signed.

Looking at them both, I said, "Thank you for allowing me to enter this dispute. I have to speak to the other party and make sure that she is aware that I have assumed this position and will be working with all of you." Turning away from them, I winked at Juan and nodded, saying, "I'll be up in the jury gathering room."

When entering a dispute, it is vital to give the parties a chance to allow you in. Otherwise you are an intruder and, hence, a potential enemy.

I found the woman sitting where I had left her in the hall. She was reviewing her papers and looking resolute.

"Well, it looks as though they are going to allow me to mediate this case," I said. "I'd like to do this individually, in a caucus style."

Before I could explain further, she said, "I understand that. I'm a paralegal, and I know the court system."

I continued, "I'd like to take you upstairs to the jury gathering room. It's quieter there and the chairs are much more comfortable." She nodded her head in agreement.

The defendants were on the first floor and the plaintiff was on the third. Everyone was simmering down, and I was allowed into the leadership role. After the initial conflagration, things were looking up.

The jury gathering room was empty, and we found a comfortable spot to sit.

"I'm sorry that you have had to go through this. I'm just becoming acquainted with your case. If you don't mind, could you tell me what this is about?"

The woman read from her notes in a calm voice. As I took my own notes, she continued, "They sold this car to me and the car didn't seem to run right. I complained to them about it both by phone and by these letters. I then had the car checked out by an independent auto repair shop. Here are the reports about that."

I held up my hand. "Please tell me more about what happened."

She continued, "I complained to them about the problems and sent them the report from the other repair shop that showed all the things that were wrong with the car that they hadn't disclosed to me.

I don't know if I even *want* the car anymore. I'm a paralegal. I work with attorneys and I know my rights and the law."

She continued her explanation for about ten minutes. I said, "Thank you. I understand much more now. I think I'd better go downstairs and find out what's going on. I may be away for fifteen to twenty minutes. Are you going to be all right up here?"

With a hopeful look she replied, "Yes, of course."

I headed downstairs to the jury room, hoping that everyone truly had calmed down.

Entering the jury room, I could see that Juan had been doing his part to contain and calm the other party.

I smiled reassuringly and sat down. "Well," I said, "I'm glad we are going to be able to do this mediation. I really think that we can get something done here. I've talked with the other side, but I haven't heard what is going on with you yet. Can you tell me what happened?" I was positively reinforcing the mediation process.

The husband began. "We own an auto dealership that specializes in used autos that we inspect, repair, and resell. We have been doing this for more than fifteen years, and occasionally we run into something like this. I think it's just buyer's remorse that she is feeling."

He then described his business, glancing at his wife who nodded in agreement. They had started the business after coming to this country following the fall of the Shah of Iran, and had spent years rebuilding their lives, which had included forming this business. He did the buying and selling, auto auctions and managing the dealership. She administered the business, did the books, and raised the family. Both of them worked with diligence and dedication.

The man started to veer from his explanation, using longer pauses and looking at Juan, the other mediator, for help.

I turned to Juan. "Juan, while I was gone, you've been talking with these people. What do you think is going on here?"

"Well, I think that the buyer didn't think she had gotten a good deal. It would seem that their paperwork is in order … although it would have to be the judge who decides that."

Juan then explained the timing of what had happened, adding the fact that the car had been repossessed and towed from the plaintiff's driveway at 5 a.m. on a workday morning. The plaintiff had come out of her house screaming, and the tow truck driver had said a few words to her about people who didn't pay their bills.

It sounded like a case of adding insult to injury.

I sat at the head of the table with the man on my left, his wife beside him and Juan sitting on my right.

As I settled back in my chair and relaxed, I leaned slightly over toward the husband. He followed suit, leaning closer to me.

I said, "I can understand that you're upset. You did all you could to help this person keep her car."

His wife suddenly spoke up with an irritated tone. "Tell him all about it."

He held up his hand for her to stop. "Emma, we talked about this. Please be quiet."

She was not at all happy.

I looked at him and said, "Your wife handles the paperwork?"

He nodded yes.

I continued, "Perhaps we should hear from her since it is the paperwork that will provide the evidence which might make the difference in this case."

As the mediation progressed, the man and I had gradually moved closer to each other, like two conspirators. Placing my hand gently atop his, I said, "Please, I'd like to hear her."

He nodded his assent.

Emma, feeling acknowledged, straightened proudly in her chair. "I do handle all of the paperwork and money for this company."

She went on to explain both her job duties and the bills that were outstanding. I was impressed. She was exact with the dates and billed amounts, and she had copies of all the correspondence and other relevant paperwork as well as a listing of their rights under the law.

Her file was so large that I commented, "That looks like a lot of work you have had to do." Apparently, this was the recognition that she needed.

Emma snorted, "Yes, that ..." — her lips compressed into an angry fine line — "was faxing me fifteen to twenty times a day, and I answered every single one! I would spend almost my entire day answering her faxes!"

I sat forward, looked down at the table, brought my right hand up to my forehead, shook my head slowly, and sighed. Looking over at the husband, I asked, "Do you know what that woman was doing?"

He answered, "Ruining my life?"

"No, she was wallpapering."

"What do you mean?"

"Wallpapering. It's a business technique or strategy where you send many faxes, maybe twenty per day, to overwhelm the other party with paperwork that they have to answer."

It was clear to her husband now just how much tiresome work this one deal required and that he had not given his wife appropriate recognition.

With such built-up anger and frustration, it's no wonder it had all seemed to explode when they finally confronted the buyer that morning. Now, however, the wife saw that it had not been a personal assault, but a clever business strategy.

More importantly to Emma, her husband now finally understood the paperwork assault to which she had been subjected and how hard and diligently she had worked in the interests of their business. As this realization sank in, he looked down at the table and slowly shook his head.

Leaning back in my chair, I said, "I need to go back upstairs. Is there anything that we have discussed that I cannot share with the other party?"

Both shook their heads no, so I headed back up to the third floor.

Going over to the woman sitting in the sunshine, I said, "Well, they really don't want to take your car away from you. Do you really want to get rid of it?"

She was trying to make up her mind about this. She liked the car and needed it for her work. She felt that she had paid more than it was worth and was worried that the 30,000 miles guarantee was no longer any good, as the car had been repossessed. She had also already driven it more than 9,000 miles, leaving only 21,000 miles on the original warranty. Most importantly, the garage she had taken it to scared her with reports of potential future problems and projected high costs for possible needed repairs.

In addition, one of the attorneys she worked for had told her that he would work at a discounted rate to support her claim should it go to civil court.

"You have to decide if you want the car, or even if it's worth it to you to keep it. I'm just here to help form some kind of agreement, if that's possible. I don't want to convince you to do anything other than what you think is right for you. I've seen the paperwork that the other party brought, as have you. Do you think that they will prevail in court? You are a trained paralegal, so you would have a better idea than most." I continued, "These people have been doing this business for years. Do you think their paperwork is out of order?" I paused. "What is it that will really fulfill your wants and needs?" We had trust and understanding between us at this point, and she was ready to answer this question.

She smiled tiredly, reconsidering. She had seen their paperwork, and she had thought about the car. "Well, I really need the car for work" — she was at a turning point, realizing she could lose everything — "and I would be willing to settle, but I need the car back and the guarantee that it will still be under the remaining warranty."

"Are you willing to pay them the balance on the note they hold on the car?" I asked.

"Yes, as long as there are no late fees and that the car is returned in good condition and that I have my guarantee for 21,000 more miles." Thinking about it further, she added, "*And* that I get it back by next week." I noted her stipulations and headed back downstairs.

As I returned to the jury room, the man looked up at me and smiled for the first time, saying just said one word, "Wallpapering."

Sitting down next to him I smiled back, chuckled, and nodded.

Leaning back in his chair, hands behind his head and smiling, he looked at his wife. "Wallpapering," he said to her, and she smiled back.

The transition, or sticky point, had been passed when the husband and wife were together in understanding. They agreed to accept the conditions of the other side. We wrote up a tentative agreement, making note of areas that still needed some work. Juan and I went back and forth between the parties discussing the possibilities with each party and modifying the agreement until we had a deal fully ironed out.

By this time, almost two hours later, both parties were ready for an end to the conflict. I brought the plaintiff back to the jury room. I seated the parties across from each other and had Juan read the Mediated Agreement, which all parties signed.

After he had finished with this part of the process, I spoke again. "I realize that this has not been easy for any of you." Glancing at both sides of the table, I continued, "I want to make sure that this matter is put to rest so that all of you can move forward with your lives. We have formed a legal way to do that, but will you please shake hands on this deal?"

Both parties stood up and, reaching across the table, they all shook hands.

After reaching agreement, the defendant phoned his cousin who had towed the car and arranged for the car to be cleaned and towed back to the woman's house the next day.

One of the major sticky points here was the dissension created between the husband and wife by the plaintiff's use of the wallpapering strategy. The fighting that had been going on between them was a consequence of this manipulation and had occurred within the bounds of doing business. It was not a personal assault. They could now laugh at the situation. The wife had done everything possible to ensure the safety of the family and the business. When the husband understood this, the family was again at peace. It was by dealing with this emotional component of the conflict that they were ready and able to come to a non-emotional decision.

In this case I used the evaluative model of mediation, helping the plaintiff conduct a risk assessment of what she stood to lose. The defendants' paperwork to repossess the vehicle seemed to be in order. Her own paperwork listing projected repair costs, on the other hand, was based on mere speculation of non-existent future problems, which might not stand up in court. And she had, after all, purchased a used vehicle. This conversation provided the transitional moment at which she realized that she might not prevail should her case go before a judge, and she did indeed need her car. She was able to see clearly, through the process of mediation, that agreeing to a compromise was, indeed, her best option.

FROM THE TOOL BOX

1. Calm behavior on the mediator's part establishes a peaceful setting that encourages compromise. I have even taken a party for a walk to help shift tension.

2. Using the evaluative technique of risk assessment can help each party understand all options and help to fully address wants and needs.

3. Notes are important in mediation. Note-taking helps the mediator understand and follow the mediation. Parties understand that their words are important, heard, and recorded. Occasionally, the mediator's notes can be used for clarification purposes. Notes *must* be kept in the mediator's possession when going into caucus.

UH-OH!

I have often found that there are negative transition points in relationships that can create conflict between people. They are most often caused by misunderstanding in communication, the feeling of personal insult, or by one party inflicting pain on another in answer to their own pain. In the mediation process these are often points that, if found and brought forth, can provide greater understanding and forgiveness and the option for people to move forward with their lives. In this case a simple miscommunication between the parties caused the dramatic events that brought them to court.

The afternoon calendar was a full one, and I was placing the mediators into the two courtrooms we were using that day. For more than two years mediators had been coming in and helping the court system, and we had now become an accepted part of Small Claims Court. The group had a great success rate, and, if nothing else, mediation gave the disputants a chance to better understand their cases and release some of their emotions.

The case that I received involved a homeowners association (HOA) and one of its members. We were seeing many of these cases in court as a result of the subprime mortgage crisis of 2008. An association's loss of dues from foreclosed members made the remaining owner members responsible for making up the shortfall, and as foreclosure rates grew, the amounts could be sizable. Having an owner's rate rise from a few hundred dollars to a thousand dollars could make the difference between successful ownership and foreclosure. Should one owner vacate, the remaining homeowners had to pay the increased dues to protect their own monetary property interests. It could be a bad situation all around.

On this particular Friday we had so many mediation cases that all the rooms we usually used for mediation were full. Rumor had it that the mediators were doing almost as many cases as the judges, and I was allowed to use the judge's chambers and law library to deal with the case overflow. The judge's room was a quiet place and the library next door had a round table and chairs around it. A skylight provided a warm, natural light, and bookshelves full of law books spoke silently of the room's usual, more studious purpose.

Two of the plaintiffs were the HOA officers: the president, a middle-aged white man dressed in slacks, sports jacket and no tie, and the secretary, a resolute older white woman dressed appropriately for court and carrying a large stuffed briefcase. The third plaintiff was an older white man dressed in a very well-cut three-piece suit and tie. He looked vaguely familiar to me. Where had I seen him before? The defendant was a Hispanic woman dressed casually but neatly. She sat sullenly, avoiding all eye contact, and slumped defensively in her chair. Clearly, she did not want to be in court.

She's angry, I thought. *I'll need to get to the bottom of this.*

I gathered the parties around the table, with the defendant on my right and the association president and secretary on my left. They all sat down purposefully and efficiently, the secretary digging out a stack of papers from her black leather briefcase. The man in the beautiful suit had taken a chair behind me. I wondered why.

I started my introduction process, which by now had become almost automatic, giving me mental space to observe the parties closely. The president and secretary looked straight at me with a businesslike earnestness, while the defendant peered at the table, her lips slightly pursed.

She's __really__ angry, I thought.

"Thank you for agreeing to take part in this process," I began. "I always find it best to establish how each party wants to be addressed. My name is Will."

Signaling to my left, we started.

"My name is Bill. I'm the president of the Association."

"My name is Claire. I'm the secretary of the Association."

"My name is Maria. I used to own the unit." Now I could tell something of the source of her anger.

Turning in my chair, I looked inquiringly at the man behind me.

"My name is Thomas." He gave his last name, too. "I am a member of the board."

"You look familiar," I said.

"Why, yes," he said importantly. "I am a trial attorney at this courthouse, and I am very familiar with our rights in this case. I'm here to make sure they are maintained."

Okay, but I'm not going to let you ambush me from behind, I thought defensively to myself. But the words that came out of my mouth were gentler. "Well, thank you for being here. Won't you please come up to the table and be part of this process?"

Grudgingly, he scooted his chair up to the table.

With this situation, I would need to lay some firm groundwork. As he settled in his chair, I made firm eye contact. "As I'm sure you know as a member of the Bar, there are no attorneys allowed in Small Claims Court." I needed to make sure he would not try to wear his attorney hat during this process.

He nodded his assent.

With my leadership of the process firmly established, I continued my standard introduction to the group. "Mediation is a process of exploring the options available to all of you in this dispute." The ground rules were set, the process explained, and the documentation exchanged.

The president and the secretary started by explaining their case. The defendant had left more than a year of fees unpaid during an attempted renovation and then the foreclosure of her property. It amounted to thousands of dollars. In addition, there were charges added for all the secretary's time handling the paperwork involved in the dispute. The association had already filed liens on the property and approached the unit's lender and arranged to take over the property as the paperwork came through on the foreclosure.

After they had finished, I turned to the defendant. "Maria, could you please tell us your side of this?" I asked. She was still slumped in her chair, tight-lipped and containing her anger.

"These people are bad people."

The member of the board snorted.

Holding up my hand, I said sternly to them both, "I will allow no disrespect at this table. We all have agreed to that." They nodded their acquiescence.

She continued, "I've lost my house and everything I put into it to foreclosure. I've had to go and start a new life, and now all they want to do is get more money from me. But I don't have it."

She then talked nostalgically about the home that she had owned and how she had lost it. She recounted how she had been remodeling one of the bathrooms to get the unit ready for sale, and how she had tried to work with the HOA. The Covenants, Conditions and Restrictions (CC&Rs) which govern an owner's actions and rights in the ownership of his property made it necessary for the association to inspect any work done and to provide licensed plumbers, approved by the association, for plumbing work. She had contacted the HOA repeatedly to request a plumber, but their plumber never contacted her. Finally, she hired another plumber who came and did the work. However, the association would not give their approval because one of their plumbers had not done the work. The association then contacted the City Building Department to file a formal complaint against the property owner. When the prospective buyer, whom the defendant had found, learned of this complaint, he backed out of the deal. Maria felt that they had forced her to lose her home.

She summed up her hardship story with resolute determination. "I don't want to be around these people. No house is worth that."

Where was the transition point? Where did things turn sour? I needed to answer these questions to uncover the key to resolution. I decided to use the reflective summation technique to find out.

Sitting back in my chair and taking off my glasses, I rubbed my eyes and started.

"Maria, I'm very sorry you have lost your home." I paused for a moment to acknowledge the difficulty she had been through.

"I think if it is all right with everyone, I would like to track through what happened. It will help me understand. Can we do that?" Asking permission always helps smooth the mediator's path. They all agreed. The secretary pulled out her logbook of calls, the president put his notes in order, and the board member sat back in his chair. The defendant took out her notes, betraying a slight glimmer of hope as she began to engage actively in the process.

I then went through the dates of each interaction and the events that had led up to them. "Okay, Maria, you informed them on that Thursday that you wanted to do the work on the bathroom?"

Maria nodded.

And so, the process went, day by day, piece by piece, tracking every component of the bathroom renovation process — wood framing, electrical, sheetrock — until we came to plumbing. The secretary had done a very good job. Each call in and out of the HOA was recorded. We finally reached the point in our review where the HOA should have called the plumber to have that work done. The request from Maria was there, but nothing else.

"Yes," Claire said, "the log book shows the call in but no call out to our plumbers."

Claire looked concernedly at Bill. "Uh, Bill, I have no record that we ever called one of our plumbers." She quickly shuffled through the following pages. "Yeah, we never called a plumber," she said in a falling tone.

Ah, the negative transition point.

I heard a sharp intake of breath on my left. Glancing over at the board member, I saw he looked stunned, his preconceived plan shattered in an instant.

I jumped in. "If I understand this correctly, you were both working well together on this project until this point. There was a lack of communication that took place, and from then on it just got worse. Is that correct?"

Bill and Claire, looking at the table, nodded. Maria, looking up for the first time, nodded yes. The board member was very quiet, looking down at the table in silent defeat.

Bill quickly spoke up. "I think we should just drop this. I want to have this case dismissed." He knew the law and knew they would have a hard time convincing a judge that they were in the right when they had obviously failed to live up to their duties.

Claire agreed in a subdued tone, "I want to, too."

The board member was undoubtedly doing a tail-between-the-legs risk assessment that may have gone something like this: The evidence shows that our plumber was never called, the prospective buyer pulls out, and we take over the property. Civil suit? Then who will have to defend the board? Me? At no cost? Uh-oh! Oh, no!

Bill and Claire looked over at him. He sat back and nodded with a cross-armed sigh, acknowledging their loss and agreeing to the plan.

I wrote up the mediated agreement to have the case dismissed. As per each side's request, I included that there would be no further legal action taken by either party against the other regarding this. Maria was happy because she was finally heard. She would no longer have to endure contact with these "bad people," and she could at last start putting her finances back together and move on with her life. Bill and Claire were happy because the HOA would no longer have to deal with this issue or any liability from it. And the board member? Well, he was the last to sign. Leaning over next to him, I offered him my pen, and pointing to the line on the document, I said, "Here, sir. You sign right here."

Reflective summation proved to be the most powerful technique in this conflict. The process of walking the parties, step by step, through the events helped uncover the exact point of confusion and miscommunication — the precise point where "things went bad." The reflective summation technique is useful in a variety of conflicts and is especially useful in family conflicts where the conflict may have started years earlier.

Another part of the process was to get all the parties in the room to the table and designate their respective roles. This helps establish the positions and responsibilities each party holds. By bringing the board member to the table, he became part of the process.

FROM THE TOOL BOX

1. Reflective summation creates a timeline of actions and events that all parties can agree to.

2. Bringing *all* the parties to the table enables them to create a collaborative environment to work within. If all the parties know the parts they play, then all can work together.

3. My recognition of Maria's pain helped create a feeling of empathy by the other parties at the table. Her release of pain and the others acknowledging their part in it created understanding.

PIXIE DUST

Some weeks before, one of the court clerks had pulled me aside and asked, "What are you doing in there, man? We court clerks have been keeping track of you. You're at a ninety eight percent success rate." I could only answer, "Well … I listen to them man, you know … connect as a person and help them out of their conflict." I wondered again if there was a "pool" going on. It had become obvious that I had become a topic of discussion. Me, I'd just rather do the job I loved doing and not worry about success rates.

It was a hot summer day and the downstairs courtroom had more than thirty cases, with an additional thirty cases moved to the upstairs overflow courtroom where I was working. Karen, the court's mediation program director, had taken over downstairs. She was my boss and, thankfully, always completed all the administrative work, leaving me free to focus exclusively on the mediations.

As I walked into the courtroom, I heard David, the court clerk, say loudly, "Well, he's here." I didn't think anything of it as I went to the jury box, where the mediators gathered. It looked like a full calendar posted in the downstairs lobby, with maybe thirty people in this court's gallery, so I thought there was a good chance I'd have a case.

It looks like everybody showed up today, I thought. We'll definitely have some contested cases.

David looked up and said, "Will, the judge wants to see you in his chambers."

You bet. Ask and I shall be there, Your Honor, I thought to myself.

This judge was one of my favorite judges, who ran his courtroom with style and grace. He was a strong judge, never losing control of the courtroom or the procedures of the court. There was never any question of where a person stood. I had never seen him pontificate from the bench, and he always explained to the disputants the reasons for his rulings. He had my respect for the ways he respected others.

Going back into the hallway leading to the judge's chambers, I wondered what this summons was about. *Oh well, there's a first time for everything,* I thought.

As I entered the chambers, the judge motioned me to a chair. "Mr. Mediator…" he began seriously, then paused with a smile.

Oh boy, I thought. *What could this mean?*

"I have a case that I would like you to do this afternoon."

"Of course, Your Honor. I'd be happy to handle it."

"Do you want to see the files?" he asked.

"No, thank you, Your Honor. I'll be happy to do the work."

I returned to the courtroom and glanced at David, whose expression clearly said, "Go get 'em!" I turned and looked at Art, the bailiff, and he was on the same page, as if he had money riding on a successful outcome. The pressure was on.

I joined the other mediators in the jury box and told them the judge had put me on a case. I was going to be busy, so they had to take care of the rest of the calendar. I felt lucky to be working with such a bright and capable group of people who could so easily take the baton. After Art, the bailiff, gave the court introduction, David, the clerk, went through the roll call and swearing-in process. He then offered the option of mediation. There was a pause as litigants considered their options. One party, then another, raised their hands, and soon the other two mediators were headed out the door with cases. I waited for the judge to enter the courtroom, knowing that he had something he wanted done.

The judge entered the courtroom. "This court is now in session," said David.

Seating himself at the bench, the judge reviewed his notes. He read off several names and case numbers and asked if the people would be willing to go to mediation.

I now realized that the plaintiffs had filed three separate lawsuits on the same defendant and the judge had bundled them together.

Oh boy, here's a new one, I thought.

I looked over at the parties. On one side was a quiet Asian man sitting with a woman, Kathy, whom I knew to be an adjuster for one of the insurance companies. Although attorneys are not allowed to represent clients in the Small Claims Court, some insurance companies might send an adjuster to help their client. Most of the time these adjusters act as counselor to the clients. In such situations, I occasionally need to remind the client that the adjuster works for the insurance company. Although I am not necessarily popular among the adjusters for pointing out these potential conflicts of interest, they respect me and I, them. We all work within the bounds of the law, and it's my duty to ensure full transparency of such dynamics during mediation.

Lin, the insurance company client, was dressed appropriately for court in slacks and long-sleeved shirt, though by his quizzical expressions he looked a little lost by the court procedures. As he struggled to follow what the judge was saying, he kept looking at the adjuster, who repeatedly nodded in understanding to the judge.

Kathy, the adjuster, seemed polished and confident in her usual black business suit, white blouse, and comfortable, low-heeled black shoes. She was a professional and knew what she was doing.

The other parties were a woman and two men. One man, who appeared to be in his mid-forties, was dressed smartly in a suit and tie. He was well groomed without seeming pretentious. The other man was casually dressed in jeans, tennis shoes, and short-sleeved shirt. He was looking around with a quizzical smile as though the whole thing amused him. He did not seem phased by the situation. The woman looked like someone who had been a flower child in the sixties: long brown hair down her back, flowing tunic, and matching slacks with a fair amount of jewelry and Birkenstock sandals. Her darting glances around the room betrayed her nervousness at being in court.

After the judge finished his instructions to the litigants, we all left the courtroom and headed across the hall. Leading them into the jury gathering room, I held the door open for them to pass me one at a time. As they did so, I established eye contact, smiled, and nodded at each one.

I gestured toward a quiet area to one side and we all sat down. In the large jury gathering room there were two other mediations already going on. It was normal business for us on a Friday afternoon, and the litigants could see that this process was not unique.

My introduction was a little different that day, since this case was essentially three cases in one.

As always, I established myself as the leader, outlining what we were going to do, what we were trying to achieve, and what my ground rules were for the process.

They all nodded in agreement. I asked how we should address each other. "My name is Will. How would you like to be addressed?"

Each plaintiff gave a short introduction.

"My name is Juan. I was driving the car." "My name is Julie. I was a passenger in the car."

"My name is Mike. I was sitting in the back seat."

The defendant said, "My name is Lin. I was driving the car that hit them."

Then it came to Kathy. She stated, "My name is Kathy Jones. I'm here to represent the insurance firm."

I smiled and said, "By way of disclosure, Kathy and I have worked together before in this court." Looking at Lin, I said, "You are very fortunate to have her here to help. She is very good."

I was telling the truth. Kathy *was* very good at her job, and I was going to need her help here. If I recognized that and gave her the room to do it, I might have an ally instead of an enemy.

"Since there are three cases here, I'd like to first find out what happened. I'd like to ask Juan, the driver, to explain that. If there are any questions, can you please jot them down, and we will address them later. Does everyone have a sheet of paper?"

I handed out paper and two pens.

Juan started, "Well, I was driving down Market Street and was stopped at the traffic signal when I was rear-ended by him."

I asked, "Was there a police report?"

"Yes, but it took them a long time to get there, and we had to move off to the side of the road."

"Did they establish fault in the report?" I asked.

"Yes, because I was rear-ended, they said it was his fault."

Kathy held up her hand. I gestured to her to speak.

"I think that we should all be aware that Mr. Gonzalez has already been paid for the damage to his vehicle, and a settlement for his related loss of income has been paid."

"Thank you, Kathy," I said. "Juan, please continue."

"Well, I've got these passengers who were injured, too. What about them?"

It was already clear that I would need to separate everyone to get to the bottom of this case. But for now, my questions would attempt to point to the gist of what had happened with each person.

I started a reflective summation, "If I understand correctly, this case involves a traffic accident that occurred on March 26 and involved two vehicles." I stated all the events thus far related, as I understood them.

"Here are copies of the police report and the diagrams showing how the accident happened." said Kathy.

The others looked at them and agreed, and yet I needed more information to figure out how this case might be resolved.

I then said, "Thank you all for being so forthcoming. I believe that the only way we will be able to proceed further is for me to handle each case separately and talk to each person individually. Is that all right with you?" I turned my palms up toward the parties in a gesture of invitation.

Lin hadn't said much, always deferring to Kathy for explanation and support. Again, he looked to her for a cue. She nodded yes, and we started the next round.

"Mike, I'd like to start with you. I understand that you have not received anything from the insurance company for any loss you suffered in this incident."

There was a simple reason why I chose Mike to go first: he was the most relaxed and had a non-defensive attitude. I felt that since he hadn't received anything, there was a chance that we could show the other parties that success was possible.

As we moved out into the hall, I held the door open for Kathy, and Lin followed with Mike behind. I had separated the parties in order to establish that these were separate cases. I also didn't want the other plaintiffs to influence Mike with comments.

I caught a faint acrid scent as Mike passed. *What did I smell there? Alcohol?*

Going out into the hall, I had Kathy and Lin sit on one of the benches in the now empty hallway. I reviewed what had already been agreed upon. I said, "Mike, I understand that as a passenger in the vehicle, you suffered a loss of income and also had medical bills to pay."

Mike agreed. In the initial exchange of paperwork, he had already shown Kathy and Lin the hospital report given to him when the accident occurred. He had also shown them the pay stubs which indicated that he had missed almost three weeks of work after the accident.

I asked, "Kathy, could you and Lin please look this over again? I want to make sure I'm getting this right. While you do this, I'd like to talk to Mike for a minute."

They both nodded, and I led Mike to the other end of the hallway.

"Mike," I began, "I noticed when we were walking out of the jury room that I smelled something like alcohol. Have you been drinking?"

Sheepishly he looked at the floor. "Yeah, well, I had a couple of pops before we got here."

"Man, do you understand what it would do to your case if the judge found out that you were drinking when you came to court?"

"Well, Juan wanted to do this. He was the one who convinced Julie and me to file separate claims and take this guy to court. I mean ... it's on the insurance company to pay for this."

Well, I thought to myself, no wonder he seemed so "happy go lucky."

Reaching into my pocket, I pulled out a tin of mints. Shaking three out into his hand, I said, "Chew these up, and we'll head back."

Kathy and Lin had been looking over the medical records. As we approached, she said, "We both agree that Mr. Smith should not have to pay for any of the medical costs involved in this incident. But we do have a problem with what he is claiming for loss of income. We would agree to a settlement by paying all the medical bills and offering a lesser amount for his loss of income."

Mike, still chewing on mints, readily agreed to the amount they gave.

One down, two to go, I mused.

Returning to the jury room, we were all smiles. I let the remaining parties know that yes, we had come to an agreement, so it was time for the next party. Mike had been the obvious party to go first, his nonchalance making him already seem willing to negotiate an agreement.

I chose Julie next, for a different reason. Her anxiousness and fear could prove to be an obstacle to successful negotiation. Mike had divulged that Juan had set this whole thing up, so Juan could be an even tougher nut to crack. I'd hedge my bets and save Juan for last.

I decided to change things up a bit by moving the location of the meeting place. Why? I didn't want them to feel that there was a predictable thing going on, and I wanted to maintain their interest. Seeing us return with smiles and an agreement had given them pause.

The spot I chose was well away from the others.

"Julie, could we do your case next? I'd like to do it right over here at these tables next to the vending machines, all right?" She agreed.

The four of us were seated around one of the white plastic tables in the vending machine area.

To start off on hopeful footing, I began by mentioning the success of the last negotiation. "We have just completed the first agreement in this case. Julie, I understand that you also have not received any compensation for injuries related to this accident. Is that true?" She nodded in agreement.

I sometimes will repeat a question I already know the answer to in order to bring the party back to the present moment. It can also reaffirm the party's position or be used as a point of reference.

"At this point, I would like to review your paperwork again for medical costs and loss of wages."

Julie looked panicked. She produced the paperwork and signaled to me. "Could we talk for a minute?" she asked.

Excusing ourselves from Kathy and Lin, Julie and I went into the hall and walked to the far end. There we could go out on a balcony, which would put us outside in the open, fresh air.

"What's going on, Julie?" I asked as we stepped outside.

"I'm having these anxiety attacks here! My doctor has prescribed these medications for them, and I'm also wearing morphine patches to help me. This is just too much!"

Trying to calm her, I said "Julie, we're just here to try and find a way out of this that works for everyone. I've been wondering, how was it that you were all in the car together when you were hit?" I was bringing her back to the moment in question.

"Well, we're all neighbors," she started. "Juan had offered to take me to the hospital so I could renew my prescriptions. Mike was just hanging around and decided to go along."

The story that unfolded was one of neighbors being good to one another. I found nothing out of place. They had been neighbors in the same apartment complex for several years. As good neighbors do, each would watch out for the others and help in times of need. They had achieved an extended family relationship with common daily routines, and the accident, coming out of the blue, had disrupted their routine.

"Juan was so upset about his car," she related. "He just couldn't get over it."

She was now calm. Maybe the meds I had watched her sneak when I had come back from the first case had kicked in, or perhaps the patch she had put on before court was having its effect. I asked her what outcome she was looking for.

"I'd just like to be done with this," she said.

"Julie, what do you think should happen here?" I asked.

"Well, I want out of this. I've been through a lot, and I think the insurance company should help out here."

I nodded, waiting for her to continue.

"I mean, he did rear-end us. We were just stopped at the light."

I nodded again, encouraging her to keep speaking.

"And there was a police report. He was at fault!"

I nodded again and shared my thoughts. "Well, yes, I understand what you have told me. My concern at present is that you are well and not distressed or suffering from anxiety attacks. Are you going to be all right?"

She smiled and nodded her head and we spent a few minutes just sitting calmly and quietly. Julie then looked at me with confidence and nodded that we could proceed.

We returned to the jury room. Kathy stood up and motioned me to the side of the room. "Will, we know that she has a prescription for morphine, as well as other drugs, and is on disability."

I nodded.

Kathy said, "I want to talk to her … in caucus … privately."

I simply said, "Will you be kind with her?" This was the moment of truth, and I needed her assurance that she would do the right thing.

"Yes, I will be kind with her. Will you allow it?"

"I will be at the table next to you. I'll be there in case she has a problem with what is going on." Looking Kathy straight in the eye, I said, "If you threaten her in any way, I will be right in your lap. Do you understand that?"

Looking me back in the eye, she nodded in definite agreement.

I will not have any parties harmed at my table.

"Julie, the adjuster has a couple of questions she'd like to ask in order to fill out the papers for your claim. Would that be okay?" Julie came over, and the two women sat in conference.

I was seated at the next table with my back toward them, listening carefully and remaining vigilant.

From my viewpoint, there was no disruption or dissent or any mention of drug use. At any rate, I never had to intrude, and felt lucky that things were going so smoothly.

After a short time, they both rose and informed me that they had reached an agreement. Julie would receive compensation for all medical costs involved with the accident, and a lesser amount than she had asked for on the loss of income since she was on disability.

Two down and one to go, I thought. Juan was the last party and, as I now understood, the initiator of the court filings. I approached him next.

"Juan, could we please talk outside in the hall?"

By this time the other mediators had finished their cases, and the jury gathering room was clearing. We both noticed that there had been successful agreements reached in the other cases around us.

Cool. He's seeing that this does work for two out of three here.

Could this be the hat trick? I crossed my fingers. It seemed to me we were on a roll.

Juan and I went out to the hall, and, walking to the doors that led to the balcony, I said, "Juan, I understand that you probably feel at least partially responsible for what happened. I mean, you were driving the car that was hit."

He nodded yes.

"I'm also aware that you've received compensation for your losses." Sitting on the bench next to the windows, the sunlight was fading but still warming the spot, and it was a gentle place to sit. I wanted him to relax. I finished up. "Juan, why have you brought this to court?"

He sat in the sunlight and relaxed. The moment had come for his truth to come forth.

"Well," he said, "It didn't seem right that Mike and Julie should get nothing out of this. I helped by advancing them a couple hundred dollars. But he did hit us, and he really screwed up their lives and my car."

"Juan, can you tell me about the car?"

He unfolded his tale. It was a Mercedes Benz, with less than 50,000 miles, a 500 series, and he had bought it from a couple in a nearby wealthy community. They had made him promise to take care of it. They had loved it, and he did too. "It's the finest car I've ever had, and now it'll never be the same."

"I can understand so much more now. I'm a car collector." I told him the model numbers and types for several of my cars. "So, what are we to do here? If we are going to move forward on this, you need to decide. I can understand how you want to protect Mike and Julie.

It sounds like they are more like an extended family than anything else."

He nodded yes.

"So, what is the best thing to do here?" I put the ball in his court.

"They didn't give me enough for the car."

"Yeah, man, but you signed the documents. You let them off."

Staring at the floor he sighed and agreed. After a brief pause, he said, "Okay, I'm ready to settle."

We returned to the jury room, where Kathy and Lin sat with Julie and Mike. Walking up to them, I said, "Kathy, I think we can get an agreement with Juan that will settle this once and for all."

She nodded and rose from the group, and we went over to the table where she and Julie had been sitting. I outlined what I thought to be the "sticky points" in the agreement we were forming. Within ten minutes we had an agreement about what we were going to do, which included giving Juan funds to compensate him for what he had advanced to Julie and Mike, the court costs, and something for his time. While this went on, I noticed, smiling to myself, that Lin, Mike and Julie were talking like old friends.

We returned to the courtroom with three agreements in hand. I gave them to Art. He just smiled, as did David.

"This court is now in session," David said as the judge reentered the courtroom and took his seat at the bench.

The judge read each agreement aloud for the court record. He asked each party if they had been coerced or forced to enter into the agreements. He was watching me as they all said no.

As it was ending, the parties were smiling and shaking hands. Lin was telling Juan how sorry he was for hitting his car and how happy he was to be able to tell him. The judge was watching from the bench.

He said, "Mr. Mediator, I'd like a word with you."

As I said earlier, when I am called from the bench, I go. I found the judge not in his chambers but leaning against the doorjamb outside the courtroom.

"What in the world *are* you doing out there? Sprinkling them with pixie dust?" he asked, smiling and shaking his head in disbelief.

I simply answered honestly, "I just listen to them and connect with them and help them figure out what they need. Although they already know what they need, they just don't realize it."

And it's true. The job of a mediator isn't really to figure out what the parties need. It's to help the parties recognize and state their own needs.

About two weeks later I was in the same courtroom. I had just completed a successful mediation, and when all the parties had left, it was only the judge, the bailiff, the clerk, and me left in the room. David turned to the judge. "Well, Your Honor, it seems that we don't need you anymore. We'll just turn it over to Will." He smiled and winked.

I smiled, but the truth is that we each had an important purpose. Placing my briefcase on a chair and formally addressing the bench, I spoke. "Your Honor, we, the mediators, love you. I have never seen you do anything but honor your position. You always explain why you rule the way you do. You have never pontificated. If we fail in what we do, it falls to you to decide. I will always be a second to your first."

He left quickly after this, never establishing eye contact. I left quickly too.

A week later, during lunch with a mediation mentor of mine, I told her the story. She laughed, "Will, do you realize what you did?"

"Well, I told the truth," I answered.

Smiling she said, "He has probably never heard anything like that while sitting on the bench."

"Well, maybe it's time he did."

I used many techniques here, starting with gathering all three plaintiffs together for the introduction. It made them feel comfortable with their surroundings and the group. Then, by separating them, I took them out of that comfort zone into their individual conflicts.

I chose the party most likely to settle to discuss the specifics of his case first so that I could demonstrate to the others that it was a possible to reach an alternative to a court judgment. His attitude of nonchalance meant that he might be the most open to an agreement. Here, it was important to help that party realize his own position and bring him into the moment and the seriousness of being at court.

I then took who was most likely to be the toughest party, as she was shaking with anxiety. I had a much better idea of what was going on after the first case. I also had the first case to build on as a successful mediation.

Finally, I created a bond with the third plaintiff by telling him about my own personal experience with cars and appreciating his feeling of loss about his own car. This created a mutual understanding and helped him accept his loss.

FROM THE TOOL BOX

1. In recognizing the insurance claims adjuster at the outset, she became part of the team and felt part of the collaborative endeavor. She had no need to establish herself or assert her power, as there was no threat coming from me.

2. I used "staging," the choice of mediation location (or locations) and the placement of people in them, creating interest on their part. As events unfolded, they were unsure of what would happen next. This also allowed me more control of each party in relationship to the others.

3. As a mediator, you must be keenly aware of the emotion at the table. Emotion can be expressed in body language, voice intonation or the look in the eyes. When a person requests a private meeting, respect it, as you'll probably find out something of interest.

POSTSCRIPT

A mentor had told me that it would happen sooner or later. When it did, I was both relieved and pleased.

I had been invited to an afternoon lunch at a local restaurant. The man who had set it up was a longtime friend who had worked for me for several years after graduating from high school. I had watched him grow into manhood, and now some twenty years later, he had a wife, children and a career he enjoyed. He seemed to have achieved balance in his life. I was proud of what he'd accomplished and the person he had become.

We had recently reconnected with each other by phone, and I had told him about my work as a mediator. He was curious about it, so had asked me to chat with him about mediation over a lunch date with his family at a local restaurant. I wanted to see him and his family, so I had been happily looking forward to this meal.

I arrived at the restaurant early and was sitting by myself on the open-air veranda overlooking the yacht harbor. It was a beautiful day: sun shining, blue sky. I felt at peace with the world.

As I had entered the restaurant, I had noticed a couple sitting inside looking at me quizzically. I figured I was just getting the usual stares that seem to accompany my tall stature and long gray ponytail. The man stood up, walked through the door, and came over to me with a look of recognition and anticipation. I looked at him questioningly while a warm smile spread over his face.

"You don't remember me, do you?" he said. "You did a mediation case for me in the court."

I smiled. This recognition scenario is exactly what I had been told by one of my mentors would eventually happen. I had just done too many cases in public courts for it not to happen.

He reminded me of the basic features of his case, and as he did so I closed my eyes, the details gradually coming into sharper focus in my mind. He had purchased a supposedly new truck from a car dealership. However, when he went to pick it up on a late Friday afternoon, it was no longer the truck he had ordered: several components didn't work, one component was completely broken, there was a small dent in the rear quarter panel, it had been driven some 400 miles and it was dirty inside and out. The dealership shrugged off his complaints with a take-it-or-leave-it nonchalance.

"Yes … I do remember it now" I said quietly as I gave him the gist of the mediation that I recalled.

It was his turn to smile.

I explained that because the confidentiality laws are constantly being challenged in the mediation field, mediators generally try to forget the specific details of any given mediation. Generally, if subpoenaed, we prefer to be able to legitimately say that we do not recall specific details of the event.

"Well, I thought you might like to know what happened."

Indeed, I *was* interested. I always wonder what happens with a case after the parties leave court. I wrap up mediation cases with written agreements all the time, but never hear about the final outcomes. In most cases, I can only guess whether the parties followed through and resolved the conflict.

Smiling up at him, I invited him to sit next to me, saying, "Please sit down and tell me about it."

"Well," he began, "as per our agreement, I took the truck back."

Relaxing into a comfortable position, he then told the story about how the service center had treated him with the utmost respect and had taken the truck in for the work that had been agreed on. It had been there two days as per the agreement. When he returned to pick it up, the dealership manager was there and apologized for the former situation and went through the punch list with him. Everything had been completed and he was happy with the work.

He continued. "Will, they then put the truck up on the lift. They had detailed the whole undercarriage too! I could have eaten off it!" He looked down, fondly remembering his happy surprise in that moment.

Looking back up, he finished speaking with a broad smile. "I was so impressed. What had started out as a battle had ended up this way? I've got a sailboat, a forty-footer, and I invited them all out for a sail."

I was deeply touched. I nodded my head with a gentle smile as I realized the positive impact of this mediation.

He stood up and said, "I just wanted to thank you. You have made such a difference in my life."

I stood up and shook his hand. "Thank you for telling me this. I almost never know what happens."

As we shook hands he asked, "They really don't pay you for all that work you do?"

I shook my head no.

"They sure as hell should," he said with a smile as he walked back to his table.

Thank you, I thought. I've now been paid in full.

My friends arrived. They were a beautiful happy family. Armando, the young man whom I had known as a teenager, had become a grown man and father capable of taking care of whatever came down the pike. I was proud of him. We talked a bit about the work that I had been doing as a mediator. I told him how I had learned from an early age to work with change rather than against it, and perhaps that's why I enjoy mediating. It's a powerful process to help people shift.

At the midpoint in our meal, the man whom I had been talking with before returned.

"Excuse me, I just wanted to thank you again," he said to me.

Standing, I said, "It is I who have to thank *you*. Thank you so much for telling me what happened." I shook his hand again.

As I sat back down, my young friend exclaimed, "Wow! Is that what happens?"

I just smiled.

At the time of this writing, state-by-state confidentiality laws in relation to mediation are being written. Currently, some states require a mediator to be an attorney (therefore already safely guarded by confidentiality), but other states honor accredited training for non-attorneys as mediators.

I believe that mediators should be held much like psychologists, physicians and attorneys in the matter of confidentiality. This is the only way a person can trust a mediator without fear of recrimination. In some states it is mandatory that disputing parties try mediation before going to court, while in others mediation is not even recognized.

I believe that law is a fluid thing, changing as we as humans change, and, I hope, improving our lives.

THE TOOL BOX

While conflict resolution from the outside may seem like a web of complexity, all successful mediations are made up of simple common threads — gentle questions, compassion, connection and listening — that naturally, and usually easily, weave together. The following skills will help build on these foundations to bring successful mediation and resolution.

ACTIVE LISTENING

By bringing a fuller understanding of the conflict, active listening can guide your approach that can lead to an agreement.

In everyday communication most people will respond to others by relating their emotions in that moment:

- "I know exactly how you feel."
- "Yes, that happened to me," often followed by a story.

Emotive words and inflection can also trigger a response.

- "You SOB, I'm gonna get you!"
- "I'm so happy to see you! I've missed you so much!"

Reaction to conversation is one of the ways we communicate our feelings.

Active listening is an invaluable tool that goes beyond these standard methods of communication. In lieu of reacting, when using active listening I focus intently on the content, voice use and underlying emotions that are being expressed rather than on my own feelings. I can then tune in to the party's emotions by noting, but not reacting to, my own emotional perspective to gain a firmer understanding of the conflict.

All conversation will have components of personal identifiers such as culture, education and affiliations. These can be used as points of connection to the party to establish common ground, thus creating a gateway to shared acknowledgement and understanding.

THE OPEN-ENDED QUESTION

Whereas no one likes to be told what to do or think, skillful questions can open a door, guiding a person to think more deeply and to arrive at his or her own conclusions.

The mediator must be genuinely caring and compassionate when asking these questions. Such a curious and positive demeanor on the part of the mediator creates an awareness that can make parties receptive to change. Open-ended questions also promote a fuller engagement in the mediation process.

I frequently use several kinds of open-ended questions in my mediations. The sample questions below are only a fraction of the possibilities.

The question that nurtures — the mediator acknowledges the feelings of the parties:

- "Are you okay?"
- "I sense some pain there ... how can I help you?"
- "Should we take a break?"

The question that leads to understanding:

- "As we've been talking, I'm wondering what you think would be the best solution?"
- "What do you think will happen if you decide to do that?"
- "I think I hear some anger there. Is that true?"
- "And then what happened?"

The question that joins the parties in the process:

- "Thank you. I understand so much more now. What do you think is the best action for both of you?"
- "What should, or can, we do?"

The question that facilitates a deeper perspective of the conflict — the mediator actively tries to get opposing parties to see things from the other side:

- "If you were the other party and were faced with this situation, what would *you* want?"
- "If you were in their shoes, what would you need?"

The question that facilitates compassion and empathy — the mediator connects the parties emotionally:

- "How would you feel if that's what happened to you?"
- "Given what you know now, how do you feel about this?"
- "How do you think *they* feel about this?"

The question that breaks a loop — the mediator sees a repetitive, stagnant or resistant thought pattern:

- "I've heard you say that several times now. What do you mean by that? I really want to make sure I understand."
- "Are you sure that's what they meant?"
- "Can we go over the facts here?"

REFLECTIVE SUMMATION

Reflective summation is a powerful tool in mediation that can help get to the heart of the conflict. It is a simple tool whereby the mediator repeats back to a party what he or she understands has been said. This process provides a real chance to get the party involved in the process, allowing him or her to hear how the story sounds to others. This process can foster a deeper understanding. Some of the methods I use here are word choice, vocal pitch and body language.

By bringing a calm manner to the table I can set a relaxed atmosphere for others to match. I can also express urgency or surprise, getting the parties' attention. In gentle (or sharp) hand gestures I can display understanding, acceptance or a sense of "Whoa! Put on the brakes!" Leaning forward, I can get attention. Sitting back, I provide more space for others. These subtle movements influence the parties' responses.

I use voice tempo in combination with body language. A soft, reasonable tone will engage, while a more direct tone can instruct and a hard tone can challenge.

The pacing of the statements or questions is also important. Slow, thoughtful statements will dial down the conversation while a rapid-fire pace will dial it up.

This tool allows me to bring up important discussion points, presenting either a calm center or a cliff's edge, engaging the parties fully in the process.

You can start reflective summation with a few key phrases, such as:

- "If I understand this correctly …" — you then provide story details as you understood them.
- "Then we are agreed that this happened …" — and, again, you give the details. This both ensures your own understanding

and can bring opposing parties onto the same page about the conflict.

- "I understand that [the sequence of events] happened. What do you think should happen next?"
- "It seems to me that the important points are these ..."

THE EVALUATIVE TECHNIQUE

The evaluative technique entails positive and negative assessments of the parties' positions.

This involves walking the parties through a subjective analysis of each issue presented in the conflict. The parties can then better understand each of their current positions as well as their options for moving forward.

This evaluative analysis also fosters deeper engagement in the mediation process by providing insights into what might be the cause and circumstances of the conflict. It can also offer a different perspective.

As always, the mediator must be genuinely caring and compassionate when asking evaluative questions, rather than asking them in a way that suggests only one possible "valid" response.

Risk or Negative Assessment

Once parties have stated their positions successfully, risk assessment helps them analyze their positions as well as their needs in relation to the possible outcomes of the case.

A few examples of risk assessment lead-ins are:

- "Let's spend some time and figure out how much this will cost ..." (The cost could be in terms of time, money, safety or other factors.)
- "Given what you know now, what do you think the other party wants or needs?"
- "If you follow that path, where do you think it will take you?"

Positive Assessment

Positive assessment is a tool whereby the mediator actively reflects on the forward progress of the case. Such reflection can help focus all parties, thus promoting continued work, focus and hope for resolution. Examples include:

- "Well, as we can see, you are coming out of this with more than we had originally thought."
- "Thank you all for all the hard work that we have done."
- "Once this matter is settled, you will no longer have to deal with it."

TRANSITIONS

Mediation is based on a series of transitional steps, or emotional shifts, that lead to an understanding and acceptance of events. These transitions are simply points at which a person comprehends his or her own position in a different way.

In relating the story of the conflict, both positive and negative emotional shifts occur as the parties express their "truths." Generally, there is a negative emotional response to what has happened and a positive one when the mediation process helps parties achieve understanding and acceptance.

The mediation process even starts with a series of positive transition points, beginning with asking each party to agree to have the case mediated.

- "Hello, I have been contacted by [the other party] and they would like me to mediate this case. Are you willing to do that?" *Recognition of need is the first agreement.*
- "My position as a mediator is to help you solve this case. Are you willing to sign a document, an Agreement to Mediate, to do this?" *The willingness to act is the second agreement.*
- "Thank you for choosing mediation to settle this dispute. I would now like to have a confidential discussion about your case so that I can understand and help you." *Active participation is the third agreement.*

Starting the mediation process with positive agreements helps to create a pathway for future positive transitions.

Know that there will be also be negative transitional shifts due to emotions such as indifference, sadness or rage. These are challenges that must be addressed to bring understanding to the table.

Party's statement: "I don't want to do this."

The mediator's potential answer: "I am sure you don't, and I can understand why. This is not an easy thing to do or any fun at all, but do you think it will just go away?"

Party's statement: "Why did they do this?"

The mediator's potential answer: "I am unsure of why, but in this process of mediation there is a very good chance we can find out."

Party's statement: "I hate them!"

The mediator's potential answer: "I am very sorry that it has come to this. My role here is to help achieve understanding. Perhaps we can talk about why you hate them."

All these feelings are valid for the party at that moment in the conflict. As the party dissipates emotional energy, the mediator must actively practice a neutral stance. These expressed feelings are important and intriguing as they can provide deeper insights into the causes of the conflict. In bringing emotions forward for discussion, it is possible to create understanding of the events at their root.

THINKING OUTSIDE THE BOX

After all parties have dispelled the personal energy of their position, ask key questions about their needs and priorities to help them reach a resolution. Think about all the factors involved in the conflict. Brainstorm. Leap cognitively among primary needs and possibilities. Mentally stretch. Think creatively.

Use your full understanding of the parties, their personalities and their propensities. Use your own full toolbox of life experiences. *Then* help them sculpt a unique solution to their conflict. Always remember the diversity of the parties involved in terms of socio-economic factors, age, race, cultural background or the environment they were raised in or live in.

*   *   *

By melding or blending the tools presented here and in the previous sections, the mediator provides a safe environment for parties to express opinions and emotions fully, without interruption.

The deeper your understanding and knowledge of how people function and relate to one another, the more enlightened your approach can be.

SHIELDING YOURSELF FROM CONFLICT

You as the mediator must be ever aware of the toxicity of conflict. When working with people in conflict, you will observe and feel the emotions of all involved in the process.

As a mediator you must remember that the conflicts are the parties' conflicts, not yours. You enter into the discussion, help them define their needs, facilitate connection between them and help them come to an understanding. Use your personal feelings only to help understand and relate to the parties, free from personal judgment. You are the neutral and are there only to help establish middle ground.

In the psychological community there are methods such as support groups or consultations with colleagues to deal with exposure to negativity, but no such formalized support networks exist yet for mediators. I have asked other mediators for ideas on handling this problem. One colleague uses daily bike rides and meditation to stay balanced. Another mediator practices yoga, knits and takes long, quiet walks. Yet another uses prayer and forgiveness practices to help stay centered. And another creates wonderful gardens.

I have personally found debriefing with my fellow mediators to be extremely valuable. These discussions allow me to "unpack" the emotional load of the high-conflict situations I encounter as a mediator.

I also maintain my many other areas of interest including reading, research, writing, car collecting, project planning and the study of history. Having active outside interests fosters my own sense of wellbeing and helps ground me to maintain my own sense of balance.

As a mediator, you are in a powerful position. You hold the potential to increase understanding of past events, bringing deeper understanding to the present that can affect the future, perhaps for generations to come.

Create beauty from chaos, be the peacemaker and you will find rewards that money cannot buy.